By the hard work of others, we are led
to the most beautiful things that have been dragged
out of darkness and into the light.
Everyone is invited to experience the light
of every age and every people.
So, let us walk hand in hand with those from every age.
Let us turn from this brief and transient time
and offer our minds and hearts to the past,
which is long and eternal.

— Seneca, *On the Shortness of Life*

THE CLASSICS CAVE

Sugar Land

In Praise & Recognition of Epicurus & Epicureanism

"O Epicurus! You who were first able to raise so bright a light from so great a darkness, shedding light on the blessings of life! . . . For as soon as your system of philosophy that arose in your divine intellect begins to proclaim aloud the nature of things, the terrors of the mind disperse and the walls of the world open wide. . . . You placed human existence from amid great waves of trouble and great darkness of the mind into a condition of tranquility and a clear light. . . . I follow you, the glory of the Greeks!"

> —Titus Lucretius Carus, *On the Nature of Things*

"The system of Epicurus is the best known of any to most men. . . . [It] is an exceedingly easy one to master. . . . Here is a famous philosopher, whose influence has spread not only over Greece and Italy but through all barbarian lands as well."

> —Marcus Tullius Cicero, *On the Ends of Good Things and Bad Things*

"In my judgment, Epicurus is the one person who has discerned the truth, liberated the souls of men from the greatest errors, and delivered to men all there is to know about living well and happily. . . . Should we not feel the greatest gratitude to him who clearly heard the voice of nature and grasped its significance so firmly and so fully that he has led all sane-minded men into the path of calm and tranquility—a quiet and happy life?"

> —Lucius Manlius Torquatus, (in Cicero's *On the Ends*)

"Mark how greatly Epicurus is admired—not only by the more educated but also by the ignorant crowd. . . . My own judgment is that the teachings of Epicurus are holy and upright."

> —Lucius Annaeus Seneca, *Letter to Lucilius* & *On the Happy Life*

"Epicurus was a man truly holy and divine in his nature. He alone truly discerned that which is noble and good, and handed them down. He was the liberator of all who associated with him."

> —Lucian of Samosata, *Alexander the False Prophet*

"The people who criticize Epicurus are madmen! I say this because there is an abundance of witnesses who attest to his unsurpassed goodwill and kindness to all men. . . . While nearly every other school has died out, the Epicurean school continues forever without interruption through countless reigns of one scholarch after another."
—Diogenes Laertius, *Lives and Sayings of Eminent Philosophers*

"The school of Epicurus is like some true republic, perfectly free from sedition, with one mind in common and one consent."
—Eusebius of Caesarea, *Preparation for the Gospel*

"I have always followed and wholly approved the authority and doctrine of Epicurus, the very wisest of men . . . [He] appeared to correct and amend the mistakes of the older philosophers and put forward his own true and certain teachings on happiness."
—Cosma Raimondi, *Letter to Ambrogio Tignosi*

"As for Epicurus, who was mostly interested in moral philosophy, he hardly addressed any particular subject in natural philosophy unless it was useful to take away terrors from the minds of men."
—Pierre Gassendi, *Life of Epicurus*

"The atomical philosophy invented and brought into request by Democritus, Leucippus, Epicurus & their contemporaries . . . in our less partial & more inquisitive times it is so luckily revived & so skillfully celebrated in diverse parts of Europe by the learned pens of Gassendus, Magnenus, Descartes, & his disciples . . . that it is now grown too considerable to be any longer laughed at, & considerable enough to deserve serious inquiry."—Robert Boyle, *Works*

"The Epicureans were more intelligible in their notion, and fortunate in their expression, when they placed a man's happiness in the tranquility of mind and indolence [freedom from pain] of body . . ."
—Sir William Temple, *Upon the Gardens of Epicurus*

"Upon the whole, if the generality of mankind were to cultivate within themselves the principle of self-love; if they were to accustom themselves often to set down and consider what was the greatest happiness they were capable of attaining for themselves in this life, and if self-love were so strong and prevalent, as that they would uniformly pursue this their supposed chief temporal good, without being diverted from it by any particular passion; it would manifestly prevent numberless follies and vices. This was in a great measure the Epicurean system of philosophy."

—Bishop Joseph Butler, 1729 *Preface to Fifteen Sermons*

"Never was philosophy less heard and calumniated than that of Epicurus. . . . He was regarded as the apologist of debauchery—he whose life was a continual practice of all the virtues, and especially temperance. . . . [He said that] happiness is acquired by the exercise of reason, the practice of virtue, and the moderate use of pleasures."

—Denis Diderot, *Encyclopedia*

"The rich and polite Italians, who had almost universally embraced the philosophy of Epicurus, enjoyed the present blessings of ease and tranquility."—Edward Gibbon, *The History of the Decline & Fall of the Roman Empire*

"I too am an Epicurean. I consider the genuine (not the imputed) doctrines of Epicurus as containing everything rational in moral philosophy which Greece and Rome have left us. . . . Epicurus [gave us] laws for governing ourselves."

—Thomas Jefferson, *Letter to William Short*

"Every age of European thought has had its . . . Epicureans, under many disguises: even under the hood of the monk."

—Walter Pater, *Marius the Epicurean*

"There is no known Epicurean theory of life which does not assign to the pleasures of the intellect, of the feelings and imagination, and of the moral sentiments a much higher value as pleasures than to those of mere sensation."—John Stuart Mill, *Utilitarianism*

"He alone—the ideal Wise Man of the Epicurean faith—will know how to live as the true artist of his own life. . . . In this present 'now,' he possesses all the conditions necessary to happiness."

—Erwin Rohde,
Psyche: The Cult of Souls & Belief in Immortality among the Greeks

"Epicurus both preached and practiced the simple life, and the cultivation of the ordinary virtues . . ."

—Harris Rackham, Introduction to Cicero's *On the Ends*

"The historical role of the theory of the division of labor as elaborated by British political economy from Hume to Ricardo consisted in the complete demolition of all metaphysical doctrines concerning the origin and operation of social cooperation. It consummated the spiritual, moral, and intellectual emancipation of mankind inaugurated by the philosophy of Epicureanism."

—Ludwig von Mises, *Human Action*

"Epicurus used science as an instrument to free men from the religious fear to which he attributed human unhappiness."

—John Burnet, "Philosophy" in *The Legacy of Greece*

"Epicureans . . . arise to be the spiritual doctors of erring humanity."

—Richard Winn Livingstone,
The Greek Genius and Its Meaning to Us

"The Epicurean ethic leads to moderate asceticism, self-control and independence. . . . The Epicurean philosophy is, therefore, not a philosophy of heroes . . . Yet . . . its attraction for certain types of men is easily understandable."

—Frederick Copleston, S.J., *A History of Philosophy*

"For Epicurus [the] exercise for death . . . becomes the consciousness of the finitude of existence that gives infinite value to each instant."

—Pierre Hadot, *Philosophy as a Way of Life*

THE BEST OF
EPICURUS

THE BEST OF
EPICURUS

The Life, Writings & Teachings of Epicurus the Greek Philosopher

The Best Parts in Translation
with
a Narrative Summary of the Rest

selected, introduced, and edited by
The Classics Cave

CAVE BEST OF SERIES
the best of the classics for today

THE CLASSICS CAVE
Sugar Land

The Best of Epicurus:
The Best Parts in Translation with a Narrative Summary of the Rest

ISBN 978-1-943915-10-1

Published in the United States by
The Classics Cave
P.O. Box 19038
Sugar Land, TX 77496
contact@theclassicscave.com
www.theclassicscave.com

The Classics Cave (the Cave) is an educational organization centered on the classics of Greek and Roman antiquity, with an emphasis on the best of ancient Greek literature. Our mission is to shine the light of the past into the present for a brighter life today. Our goal is practice—the application of ancient wisdom and ways to our contemporary lives. We publish books, develop and provide online content, organize and do outreach, and produce and distribute a variety of print and other media intended to entertain and educate, inspire, encourage, and cultivate.

Visit the Cave online (www.theclassicscave.com) to support our mission and to access a growing catalog of engaging books and other beneficial content designed for individuals, educators, groups, and all others interested in benefiting from ancient literature.

For the one entering this great work . . .
Pause for a moment before its door.

Such is the holy gift the Muses give to human beings.
—Hesiod, *Theogony*

CONTENTS

PART 5
Epicureanism as Presented by Cicero

PART 6
Points of Wisdom & Ways of Practice from Epicurus

OTHER MATTERS OF INTEREST
Related to Epicurus & Epicureanism

CAVE BEST OF SERIES
INTRODUCTION
the best of the classics for today

HAVE YOU EVER considered how many excellent works of ancient Greek and Latin literature there are to read? Think of all the significant works of poetry and prose—of all the epics, tragedies, comedies, histories, philosophies, orations, biographies, and more!

The problem, of course, is in the approach. How should you read them all? It is The Classics Cave's goal to offer a possible solution— and so the Cave Best of Series, which presents the best of an author, title, or group of authors.

Take the author, title, or group you have in hand. Of the available versions of the work, the Cave Best of Series version is unique for a few reasons. One, it is much shorter than most renditions of the work—oftentimes the number of pages totals anywhere from one-third to one-half of other versions.* Consequently, if you are pressed for time or do not know how many hours you would like to invest in reading the work, then the Cave Best of Series version may be for you.

That is not to say you will not get the whole work—the whole story or discourse or whatever the work centers on. Rather, you will get it in two forms—another unique feature of the Cave Best of Series presentation of a work. Whereas most versions offer either the whole or parts of a work (without any significant explanation of what happens in between each part), the Cave Best of Series version gives you the best or most significant parts in translation, along with a narrative summary of the rest that will tell you exactly what is going on in between. This means you will get the full content, feel, and experience of the work without missing out on anything essential.

And that's important. Unlike study guide versions that offer summary outlines alone, you will have extensive passages and narrative summaries of the whole work that will allow you to judge for yourself what is happening, what characters are central, what themes are significant, what the arguments are and whether they succeed or not, and the like—all depending on the work itself.

This is what the Cave Best of Series offers: the whole work in translated and narrative summary form, making for a relatively quick read that will let you come to terms with the work by yourself.

Not only that but there is also an information-packed introduction that is meant to draw the reader into and answer the most significant questions about the author and the work. Why should we care about *this* author and *this* work? What are the essential facts we should know? What are the work's most important ideas and themes? There is always a full exploration of these points that references the work itself as well as any pertinent scholarship.

Toward the end, there is a section presenting a "Plan of Life" (or something similar), "Points of Wisdom," and "Ways of Practice" related to the author. The latter "Ways" consist of workbook or journal-like prompts and exercises intended to motivate the reader to feel, think, and act in beneficial ways according to the author's "Points of Wisdom."

Finally, there is a unique section called, "Other Matters of Interest Related to [the Author]." It offers additional information about the author, whether a summary of the work, a cast of characters found therein, maps, a glossary of relevant Greek terms, suggestions for further reading, and so on.

In the end, when you read the work as presented in the Cave Best of Series, you will be entertained, educated, and, we at The Classics Cave hope, motivated to practice—to act in an intentional, specific manner toward a better life. With this in mind, welcome to the . . .

Cave Best of Series

the best of the classics for today

---

* Even so, whole, or mostly whole, works are sometimes included in the Cave Best of Series if the work is particularly short or the sources few.

INTRODUCTION

O green and glorious! O herbaceous treat! . . . Serenely full, the epicure
would say, Fate cannot harm me, I have dined today.

—Sydney Smith, A Recipe for a Salad

M ENTION THE ANCIENT Greek philosopher Epicurus to anyone,
and you may well be gently redirected with a few questions.
Do you mean *epicureanism*? Are you talking about gourmet food?
Are *you* an epicure? If the questions are flavored with a certain en-
thusiasm, chances are your partner in conversation may next reveal
his bona fides as a foodie. And he'll have a point. When many hear
Epicurus, they think *good stuff* and especially *good food*.

There's a simple reason why. Unless you are sitting in an under-
graduate philosophy class or browsing in a bookstore, the only time
you're likely to run into the name *Epicurus* or the term *epicureanism*
is when it is grafted onto the name of a restaurant or a specialty
store or some purveyor of fine things. For example, not far from
The Classics Cave office in Sugar Land, there is Rice Epicurean Mar-
ket in Houston. The grocery store's website insists that "Our passion is food"—which is doubtlessly an appropriate and promising
claim for a supermarket. Rice Epicurean maintains that our "sea-
food ... could only be fresher if you went out into the deep blue
yourself."

Such epicurean fish-fussing is incredibly old. Athenaeus of Naucratis, the second century AD author of the *Deipnosophists*—what may
be rendered as *The Dinner Experts*, or, we might say, *The Sophisticated
Foodies*—tells us about many "people [who] have been great epicures
about fish."[1] Their epicureanism had to do with how the fish was
treated (slaves were to wash the fish rather than rubbing it down
with oil), kinds of fish (conger and pike were considered best), and
methods of cooking the fish (boiling, roasting, and the like).

As for eateries, Epicurus Restaurant in Detroit serves "breakfast all day, and some of the biggest burgers in town." According to one report, "no matter how big your appetite, you will not leave the Epicurus Restaurant feeling hungry." To some extent, getting plenty is precisely what this kind of epicureanism—both ancient and modern—is all about. Filling up! But more than that, it is about a sophisticated *gnosis* and refined tastes. You *know* you're filling up with the best.

Athenaeus presents us with a window onto this kind of epicurean phenomenon. "The comic poets," he explains, "running down the Epicureans, attack them as mere servants and ministers of pleasure and a lack of self-control." He goes on to offer many examples. First, there is the epicurean man who compared an eel, then considered a delicacy, to Helen, the most beautiful woman in the ancient world. "But when an eel was served, a certain epicurean man . . . said, 'Here is the Helen of the feast. I, therefore, will be the Paris!'" Then there is the advice of "the epicure Archestratus" regarding what sort of pastry chef one should have on hand. He "counsels us to have a Phoenician or Lydian slave for a baker since he was not ignorant that the best bread makers come from Cappadocia." Finally, Athenaeus reports the third century BC Stoic philosopher Chrysippus' story about Philoxenus. "I know an epicure, who used to convince the cooks to set the very hot dishes before him so that he would have them all to himself." Apparently, no other participant in the feast could keep up with Philoxenus' pace of eating, so voracious and all-consuming was his appetite.

Athenaeus traces this mouthful-of-pleasure brand of epicureanism back to Odysseus in Homer's *Odyssey*. He writes that "Odysseus in Homer appears to have been the original guide to Epicurus regarding this much-spoken-of pleasure." And this makes some sense. Anyone who's ever read Homer knows the heroes all have heroic appetites for roasted meat and whole seas of wine. To demonstrate the point, Athenaeus cites Odysseus' speech to Alcinous:

As for me, I declare that there is nothing better or more delightful than when a whole people join in merry festivity together . . . while before them the table is loaded with bread and meats, and the cupbearer draws wine from the mixing bowl and pours it into all the goblets.[2]

Athenaeus finishes with Epicurus himself, assigning this declaration to him: "The origin and root of all good is the pleasure of the stomach."[3]

The problem with Athenaeus' portrayal of Epicurus and Epicureanism (or better yet, *epicureanism*, no capital letter) is that it is not exactly accurate. Not at all, in fact. Fan of a simple diet of barley cakes and water—which, he claimed, would help him compete with Zeus himself in terms of bliss—Epicurus was no *epicure*. According to professor of philosophy Dane Gordon, "His manner of life was much more like that of an abstemious monk."[4]

It's true. The historian of philosophy Frederick Copleston concluded the same decades ago. "The Epicurean ethic leads to a moderate asceticism, self-control and independence."[5] In short, Epicurus was a proponent of a deliberate way of life that would help what may be termed philosophical epicures (or Epicures) to think wisely, live well, and be happy.

WHY SHOULD WE CARE ABOUT EPICURUS?

The year was 176 AD. The Roman emperor Marcus Aurelius was in Athens after months of touring the eastern empire. Aside from being initiated into the Eleusinian mysteries with his infamous son, Commodus, and taking steps to reform the government of the city, Marcus acted to recognize the longtime influence of philosophy in Greece and the wider Mediterranean world. He thus endowed four chairs of philosophy, singling out the major schools. One endowment went to the Epicureans.[6]

The emperor's act came some five hundred years after Epicurus established his school. That's far longer than any university has existed in the United States, where Harvard, founded in 1636, is the oldest. Altogether, Epicurus' school carried on from its opening around 305 BC to well into the third or even fourth century AD.

About a half century after the emperor endowed the chair, the ancient biographer Diogenes Laertius reported that "while nearly every other school has died out, the Epicurean school continues forever without interruption through countless reigns of one scholarch after another."[7] By the early fifth century, however, the school seems to have come to an end. Writing at that time, Augustine of Hippo explained that the school's "ashes are so cold that not a single spark can be struck from them."[8] Given his own animus toward Epicureanism, he was doubtlessly not disappointed. Nevertheless, over time the school was immensely influential. According to Gordon, "Epicurus's teachings provided a philosophy of life for large numbers of people through six or seven hundred years."[9]

This brings us to the first reason why we should care about Epicurus. For well over half a millennium his teachings provided the guiding light for a great number of human souls. His was a new way of looking at things that for many could explain reality, calm fears, and provide tranquility. As the professor of classics Howard Jones tells it, "from the beginning Epicurean teaching fired the popular imagination."[10] We'll see that this was both positive and negative in terms of praise and blame. But for those who turned toward the man and his teachings and embraced his way of life, Epicurus was nothing short of "a god," a bright light shining in the darkness.[11]

Over time the light itself shone throughout the Mediterranean world. Radiating from its epicenter in Athens, followers practiced Epicureanism in the islands of the Aegean and along the coasts of Asia Minor (Turkey). Key cities were Mytilene on the island of Lesbos and Lampsacus along the Hellespont. There were also pockets of Epicureans in Syria and Egypt. Later, Epicureanism spread west to Roman Italy. By the time Marcus Aurelius endowed the Epicurean chair in 176 AD, the philosophy was the guiding light for a large number of people throughout the Roman Empire, both east and west. In later times, whether directly or indirectly, Epicureanism impacted some in the Byzantine Empire and some among the Kievan Rus, and in the West its flame was relit during the Renaissance and grew larger from the seventeenth century on.

The human dimensions of Epicureanism were equally as broad in a way that is similar, perhaps, to Saint Paul's first century AD declaration that in Christ Jesus "there is neither Jew nor Greek, slave nor free man, male nor female."[12] Epicurus invited everyone to practice his philosophy. Leontion and Themista, for example, were two women involved in the school from the beginning. Diogenes Laertius informs us that Epicurus dedicated his work, the *Neocles*, to Themista, and he wrote letters to her.[13] Themista's husband Leonteus of Lampsacus practiced the philosophy as well. Aside from free persons, slaves also participated. Epicurus' own slave Mys—his name means Mouse—joined him in his philosophical studies and way of life. As for the young, they "flocked to him," and those advanced in years found solace in Epicurus' philosophy in old age.[14] There were Greeks and non-Greeks, and those with every shade of appearance. Diogenes Laertius tells us about two men—both named Ptolemy and both from Alexandria in Egypt—who eventually led the school. "The one was black (*melas*)," he reports, "and the other was white (*leukos*)."[15] Lastly, there were the rich and the not-so-rich, the powerful and the not-so-powerful.

The first point in brief is that Epicureanism was important to many people throughout many lands over a long period of time. Just as various forms of Buddhism or Hinduism, Christianity or Islam are important for many today, so was Epicureanism the path to follow for many individuals over hundreds and hundreds of years. The question, of course, is why.

The twofold answer brings us to the second reason why we should care about Epicurus—his theoretical and practical philosophy, both of which have been extremely influential and helpful to many. Simply put, people followed Epicurus for his theoretical ideas and practical wisdom.

Theoretically, Epicurus influenced the ancient and modern worlds in two significant ways. One influence came through his method of gaining knowledge, his epistemology. We can observe this method being transmitted from his early follower and friend Metrodorus in his work *On Sensation*, through a series of other followers, including the Roman poet Lucretius, whom we will discuss in a moment, to later followers such as the second century AD Diogenes of Oenoanda, who chiseled into a long wall his proclamation of the blessings of Epicureanism, including the warning that the mind can go astray without the touchstone of the senses. A last to mention is John Locke—though, to be sure, there were many others in between. In broad outlines, we can trace Locke's "primacy of sensation in the formation of ideas" and the whole train of British empiricism back to Epicurus.[16]

The other theoretical influence came through Epicurus' natural philosophy or physics, namely, his theory about atoms and the void. It is possible that modern physics would not exist had there been no Epicurus.[17] Again, the impact began early on with his followers. The most significant person, however, was Lucretius, whom I mentioned a moment ago. It was his first century BC poem *On the Nature of Things* (*De Rerum Natura*) that spread Epicurus' vision of nature throughout the Roman world. Two centuries later, Marcus Aurelius wrestled with the Epicurean position in his *Meditations*. Regarding nature, there are just two options, he observed. Providence or chance. Order or atoms. By providence and order, he meant the Stoic view of reality, including the directing mind of the cosmos. By chance and atoms, he was referring to Epicurus' atoms randomly dancing and swerving to form whole worlds and everything therein, including human reality.

This chance-based aspect of Epicurus' philosophy made it hard for his physics to gain hold in Christian Europe, where first Platonist then later Aristotelian natural philosophy held sway. But eventually Epicurus found a champion in the sixteenth century French scientist and priest Pierre Gassendi, who defended "Epicurus against his detractors" in his book *On the Life and Morals of Epicurus*. He held on to Epicurus' atoms while positing God as their creator and mover.[18] Gassendi in turn influenced several "English scientific circles" in terms of various corpuscular theories of matter. In particular, he influenced Dr. Walter Charleton, who took on Epicurus' physics as his own. The title of his 1654 book summarizes how Charleton understood Epicurus' impact: *Physiologia Epicuro-Gassendo-Charletoniana, or A Fabrick of Science*

Natural, upon a Hypothesis of Atoms, Founded by Epicurus, Repaired by Petrus Gassendus, and Augmented by Walter Charleton. In short, Epicurus was modified by Gassendi and amplified by Charleton. Four years later Charleton published *Epicurus' Morals*.

Although there continued to be various theological objections to these theories, the newly chartered Royal Society of England defended Epicurus' ideas about the most basic parts of physical reality. Leading the defense was Robert Boyle:

> The atomical philosophy invented and brought into request by Democritus, Leucippus, Epicurus & their contemporaries . . . in our less partial & more inquisitive times it is so luckily revived & so skillfully celebrated in diverse parts of Europe by the learned pens of Gassendus, Magnenus, Descartes, & his disciples . . . that it is now grown too considerable to be any longer laughed at, & considerable enough to deserve serious inquiry.[19]

Needless to say, Epicurus' view *did* receive serious inquiry in the following centuries. As any middle school student knows, atoms still play a major role in the drama of physics, chemistry, and biology today.

But Epicurus' philosophy—his theorizing about how we know things and about the nature of reality—was not just a matter of abstract reasoning for him. Instead, his theoretical inquiries always aimed at practical results. The point: theory existed for practice. This practice and the life it shaped is what most Epicureans were interested in. Said another way, they were attracted to Epicurus' way of life and path to happiness.

Unlike today, when philosophy can be very dry and very abstract, at times seeming to have extraordinarily little to do with actual life, philosophy in the ancient world was, as Pierre Hadot put it, "a way of life."[20] Although this was true for all the major schools of philosophy, it was particularly true for Epicureanism. We see the point in each of Epicurus' major letters. To Menoeceus, Epicurus explains, "We must practice those things that produce happiness since if happiness is present, we possess everything, and if not, we do everything to acquire it." To Pythocles: "Remember that, like everything else [that is, all other natural philosophy], knowledge of celestial phenomena . . . has no other purpose than tranquility of mind." To Herodotus, he declares, "We must hold that the function of the study of natural phenomena is to clearly understand the cause of the most important things. And we must hold that blessed happiness depends on this."[21]

To the extent that Epicurus was the helper of many (in Greek, his name, *Epikouros*, means "helper" or "ally"), the one who delineated the path to tranquility and the happy life, he was, as Anthony Gottlieb terms him, a "guru" to his followers.[22] For the Greek-writing Roman satirist Lucian of Samosata, "Epicurus was a man truly holy and divine in his nature. He alone truly discerned that which is noble and good and handed them down. He was the liberator of all who associated with him."[23] For the Roman Lucretius,

> Epicurus was a god—a god, I say—who first discovered that discipline of life that is now called wisdom, and who, by the science of philosophy, placed human existence from amid great waves of trouble and great darkness of mind into a condition of tranquility and a clear light."[24]

To give one last example, Torquatus—the Roman statesman and orator, and Cicero's spokesman for Epicureanism in his *On the Ends of Good Things and Bad Things*—made the point this way:

> In my judgment, Epicurus is the one person who has discerned the truth, liberated the souls of men from the greatest errors, and delivered to men all there is to know about living well and happily. . . . Should we not feel the greatest gratitude to him who clearly heard the voice of nature and grasped its significance so firmly and so fully that he has led all sane-minded men into the path of calm and tranquility—a quiet and happy life?[25]

The same general sentiment was true for all of Epicurus' ancient followers—for Mys, Leontion, Themista, Leonteus, Metrodorus, Hermarchus, Polyaenus, Colotes, Idomeneus, among others in his original circle, as well as for Polystratus, Dionysus, Basilides, Zeno of Sidon, Philodemus of Gadara, Calpurnia (the third wife of Julius

Caesar), Plotina (the wife of the emperor Trajan), and for Diogenes of Oenoanda later on.[26]

When Epicureanism was revived in Europe and later in the United States, the general emphasis on the good life and happiness was the same. In a letter to Ambrogio Tignosi, the early Italian humanist Cosma Raimondi calls Epicurus "the very wisest of men," further stating that Epicurus "appeared to correct and amend the mistakes of the older philosophers and put forward his own true and certain teachings on happiness."[27] The Englishman Sir William Temple praised the Epicureans for equating happiness with "tranquility of mind." He took Epicurus' advice to withdraw from public life seriously when he retired "to his garden at Moor Park" and wrote *Upon the Gardens of Epicurus*.[28] In America, Thomas Jefferson averred in a letter to William Short that he was an Epicurean. Explaining his choice of philosophy, he judges, "I consider the genuine . . . doctrines of Epicurus as containing everything rational which Greece and Rome have left us." In the appended "Syllabus of the doctrines of Epicurus," Jefferson states that "happiness is the aim of life" and that "the summum bonum" —the highest good—is "tranquility of mind." Back in England, Epicureanism continued to influence the understanding of the good life through thinkers and writers such as the Utilitarians Jeremy Bentham and John Stuart Mill. One scholar sums up the influence this way: "the Epicurean promotion of happiness as the chief end of living provided support for the Utilitarian movement of the 19th century."[29] We can also detect Epicurus' influence on how to live in such disparate theorists as Karl Marx, Ludwig von Mises, and Ayn Rand.

Of course, not everyone, whether ancient or more modern, agreed with the direction of Epicurus' epistemology or natural philosophy, or with his description of the good life. Not at all. In fact, as one may well imagine, there has been a good deal of criticism. John M. Rist states that "from ancient times [Epicurus'] philosophy has aroused . . . vehement opposition."[30] This was true not only for rival schools of philosophy but also for the majority in the Christian tradition beginning with Saint Paul's encounter with certain Epicureans in Athens.[31] Marianna Shakhnovich explains that "an anti-Epicureanism stance was characteristic of the Christian tradition on the whole, both in Western and the Byzantine patristic literature."[32]

Some of the earliest criticism came from the Roman statesman and philosopher Cicero. He criticized Epicurus for introducing uncaused effects into his natural philosophy (namely, the infamous *swerve* of the atoms that *just happens*), for being sloppy with terminology and definitions (what, exactly, does Epicurus mean by *pleasure*? he asks), and for teaching that one is to be virtuous for the sake of pleasure (rather than for the sake of virtue itself, as Cicero held). At one point the muddle is simply too much, and so Cicero cries out, "What a mass of fallacies!"[33] The Christian theologian Saint Augustine of Hippo concurred with Cicero's criticism of the subjugation of virtue to pleasure. In the *City of God*, he explains that Epicurus represents "Pleasure sitting on a royal seat like some luxurious queen. And all the virtues are subjected to her as slaves, watching her every nod so that they may do whatever she commands."[34]Arguing against Epicurus a few centuries after Cicero, Plutarch wrote a short work called, *That It Is Not Possible to Live Well Following Epicurus*. Though the read is of interest, we need not go into the details since for Plutarch the title betrays the conclusion. As for Alexander, the second century AD so-called "false prophet," he believed that Epicurus' chief teachings deserved to be burned. Lucian of Samosata reports that Alexander torched a copy of Epicurus' *Principal Teachings* in a bonfire, tossing its ashes into the sea.[35]

The wide-ranging Neoplatonist philosopher Plotinus criticized Epicurean epistemology for its inability to get at the being and thus the truth of things.[36] The Platonist-leaning Augustine similarly dismissed Epicurus for identifying the "judging faculty of truth with the senses of the body." Yet this was Augustine's general criticism of Epicurus—his materialism that was "enslaved to the body," that he "conceived only of material origins for all natural phenomena . . . in the atoms, that is, in the smallest of little bodies, indivisible and indiscernible by the senses." Some materialists, he said, "like the Epicureans, believe that living things could be produced from non-living things."[37] For Augustine, the very thought was absurd. Therefore, Epicurus' whole natural philosophy was preposterous.

The early twentieth century idealist philosopher A.E. Taylor censured Epicurus for choosing his atomist explanation of nature to get rid of God. Speculating in his 1911 book *Epicurus*, Taylor asserts that Epicurus banished God not for any legitimate scientific reason but merely because he "dislikes the thought of a God whose judgments may possibly have to be reckoned with hereafter."[38] Then again, for Epicurus, there was no "hereafter" since he denied the immortality of the soul. This was another problem Augustine had with Epicurus. Epicurus would neither believe "in a life for the soul after death nor in places of recompense."[39] He wasn't the only one that judged Epicurus for his failure—or refusal—to believe in the afterlife. In the *Divine Comedy*, Dante situates all Epicureans in the sixth circle of hell for this precise reason. "Within this region is the cemetery of Epicurus and his followers, all those who say the soul dies with the body."[40]

The greatest problem that Augustine and others, including a long line of Christian fathers and later Christians, had with Epicurus was his identification—or confusion, they would say—of happiness with pleasure. The second century Clement of Alexandria accused Epicurus of "prefer[ing] pleasure to truth."[41] Augustine himself stated that "the Epicurean philosophers certainly live in accordance with the flesh since they place the highest good of man in the body's pleasure"—something that is true for most people, he claimed.[42] The latter judgment was echoed by the twelfth-century bishop John of Salisbury, who mourned that "the world is filled with Epicureans for the simple reason that in its great multitude of men there are few who are not slaves to lust."[43]

We can learn a great deal from those who criticized Epicurus. But for those who favored him and argued on his behalf, the positives ended up outweighing the negatives. More than that. Many simply shrugged off the criticisms as unfair calumny.

For instance, in his work *Utilitarianism*, John Stuart Mill argued that the various criticisms of Epicurus' teaching regarding pleasure present it as "a doctrine worthy only of swine, to whom," he went on to report, "the followers of Epicurus were, at a very early period, contemptuously likened." In defense of Epicurus and various forms of Epicureanism, Mill countered that "a beast's pleasures do not satisfy a human being's conception of happiness." While Mill conceded that Epicurus could have better expressed himself relative to the nature of and relationship between pleasure, virtue, and happiness—a criticism earlier levelled by Cicero and Seneca—he nevertheless insisted that "it is better to be a human being dissatisfied than a pig satisfied; better to be Socrates dissatisfied than a fool satisfied."[44] Presumably, Epicurus would have judged the same. Whatever the case, Mill believed Epicurus was worthy of a closer examination.

This brings us to the final point, the final reason why we should care about Epicurus. We can learn and benefit from him and his philosophy today. This doesn't mean, of course, that we have to accept everything from Epicurus. But if we pick and choose without expecting to swallow his philosophy whole, understanding, for instance, that virtue has intrinsic value or that science has advanced lightyears since Epicurus first posited his atoms and the void, then perhaps we'll be able to find something beneficial for our own lives.

We will look more at the contemporary relevance of Epicurus as we go along. For now, let's give the final words to professor Howard Jones:

> As long as individuals are intent on attaining personal happiness, as long as the prospect of death instills fear, as long as there is an urge to escape the demands of a busy world, and as long as there is debate about the origins of the cosmos, it would be surprising if the basic teachings of Epicurus did not still exercise some appeal.[45]

BASIC FACTS ABOUT EPICURUS

Early life—peace and flux. The cosmos was aligned just right when Epicurus was born. Or so Colotes, one of his original followers, declared. Plutarch quotes him as saying that Epicurus' "mother had just so many atoms within her that, when coming together, they must have produced a complete wise man."[46]

However that may be, Epicurus was born on the island of Samos in the Aegean Sea just a mile off the coast of modern Turkey. The year was 341 BC. According to the ancient biographer Diogenes Laertius, he "was born in the third year of the 109th Olympiad, in the archonship of Sosigenes, on the seventh day of the month of Gamelion, in the seventh year after the death of Plato."[47]

The island itself—Samos—is spectacularly beautiful, surrounded by a clear blue sea, the sort one may imagine sitting next to in peace all day long. We may suppose that a similar peace—the tranquility of the physical setting or something like it—was something that remained with Epicurus throughout his life, a point we will return to. The circumstances of his parents' arrival in Samos, however, must have been anything but peaceful.

Epicurus' father and mother, Neocles and Chaerestrate, arrived on Samos as cleruchs, or colonists, just over a decade before their most famous son was born. This was all well and good except for there was already a sizeable population on the island. The colonists' arrival, therefore, meant that the existing occupants had to be removed from their property and either tossed off the island or kept in subjugation. In short, it was no peaceful affair.[48] Consequently, in contrast to the island's naturally tranquil setting, the political environment was anything but peaceful. The whole affair ended some three decades after the colonists' arrival, when they were forcibly evicted from the island. But more on that in a moment.

It is usual for scholars to emphasize the changing political times into which Epicurus was born.[49] From a Greek world centered upon loyalty to what were, generally speaking, small city-states, Alexander the Great shifted focus to a much greater Macedonian Empire that was soon divided into multiple smaller kingdoms after his death. The upshot: people found themselves adrift in a great sea of political anonymity and hence, for many, political meaninglessness.

All this is true to some extent. But zooming out from those decades closing the fourth century and Alexander's sweeping moves to unify the Greeks as they had never been unified before, we see a constant flux in Greek political affairs from the early fifth century on, if not long before. It was this ongoing flux that Epicurus was born into. "Epicurus lived when very difficult times prevailed in his homeland."[50] Such was Diogenes Laertius' brief judgment. There was the glory that was Greek politics, yes, but also the agony.

Samos' own recent turbulent history reflected the flux as one people streamed in to dominate while the other receded in submission—before the tide eventually turned again. Either way, the political environment of Samos was dissimilar to the tranquil blue sea with which Epicurus was likely familiar, the calm harbor he later pictured as the happy safe haven of the older wise man's life.

When Epicurus was eighteen years old, he left Samos behind for a few years. The year was 323 BC, the year Alexander the Great died. Left behind on the island were his father and mother, as well as his three brothers Neocles, Chaeredemus, and Aristobulus. Epicurus' destination was Athens. He was going there because he, along with his whole family, was an Athenian citizen, and so he was obliged to give two years for military training and service. Benjamin Farrington tells us that those in training "were taught to fight in heavy armor, use the bow and javelin, and discharge a catapult."[51]

While Epicurus was hurling one projectile or another, his parents and brothers were being forcibly ejected from Samos by Alexander's former general Perdiccas. They landed in Colophon slightly inland along the coast of Asia Minor, about fifteen miles northwest of ancient Ephesus. Epicurus joined them there in 321 when he was twenty. His military service complete, he now turned to figuring out what to do with his life. His father was a schoolteacher; his mother seems to have worked as a fortune teller and a performer of "purificatory rites."[52] But what would he do?

Education and turn to philosophy. Diogenes Laertius relates the account of Epicurus' early disappointment with Greek mythology's actual power to explain reality. Citing Apollodorus the Epicurean, he explains that Epicurus "turned to philosophy thanks to his contempt for teachers who were unable to explain the meaning of *chaos* found in Hesiod."[53] For as Hesiod had sung in the *Theogony* nearly four hundred years before, "Truly Chaos was born the very first."[54] It's not that the young lad lacked imagination. Instead, however poetic and possibly meaningful mythical explanations were in themselves, if they were mere signs pointing to nowhere, they were useless. And as we'll see, Epicurus was very much about what was useful.

Aside from his own youthful ruminations on the nature of life and reality, Epicurus' first substantial contact with philosophy came sometime in his early teens if not slightly before.[55] The ancient author Diocles reports that Epicurus was an admirer of the fifth century BC philosophers Anaxagoras and Archelaus (the latter was Socrates' teacher).[56] If true, we have no further information. Otherwise, it is possible that Epicurus studied with the Platonist philosopher Pamphilus from when he was fourteen or so until he departed for Athens and his military service. This is what Ariston, who wrote a biography of Epicurus, reports—but again, without details.[57]

J.M. Rist tells us that when Epicurus was in Athens, he "had some opportunity to hear the major philosophers of the day."[58] According to one ancient report, Epicurus "listened to the lectures of Xenocrates," the third head of the Academy, Plato's school.[59] He may have also heard Theophrastus, Aristotle's successor. (Given the political flux of the times, Aristotle had recently departed from Athens, not wanting to appear "pro-Macedonian" in what was by then a very anti-Macedonian city.[60]) The bottom line is that we really don't know what Epicurus would have learned in Athens in terms of philosophy. It is possible that he was so busy with his military duties that he had no time for philosophical pursuits.[61]

What we do know with a fair amount of confidence is that Epicurus' life shifted significantly once he moved to Colophon. At that point, or at some point thereabouts, he encountered the philosopher Nausiphanes of Teos and his major work the *Tripod*.[62]

Epicurus learned much from Nausiphanes—much that would over time form the backbone of his own philosophical system. Diogenes Laertius gives us Ariston's report "that Epicurus' treatise called *The Canon* originated from the *Tripod* of Nausiphanes."[63] If true, then this means that Epicurus' epistemology, his system delineating what can be known and how we can learn and know about things, came from Nausiphanes. More importantly, perhaps, Epicurus learned the basics of atomism from him—the philosophy of nature positing atoms and the void that originated with Leucippus and Democritus in the fifth century BC. According to Diogenes Laertius, the ideas found in "the works of Democritus" instigated Epicurus' real turn toward philosophy.[64] Then again, he was also attracted to the goal that Nausiphanes posited for human life—that of imperterbability (*akataplēxia*). Scholars suspect that Epicurus' own stated goal of *ataraxia*—literally "lacking disturbance" or, to state it in positive terms, "calmness" or "tranquility" (as it is often given)—was inspired by Nausiphanes' *akataplēxia*. We can imagine that *ataraxia* resembled for Epicurus the clear, blue, and peaceful waters surrounding parts of Samos. Both Epicurus' and Nausiphanes' goals were likely the thought-descendants of the fearlessness or "absence of dread" (*athambiē*) of Democritus.[65]

In the end, Epicurus unearthed the building stones of his philosophy from various philosophical quarries: from the atomists, through Nausiphanes and Democritus' writings; from Pyrrho's skepticism—again, through Nausiphanes; from Aristotle's philosophy, through Aristotle's own work and that of Theophrastus and others at the Lyceum; and from the Platonists of the Academy, even if their ideas only gave Epicurus something to react against. According to Farrington, Epicurus "labored to take account in his system of the best ethical and the best natural philosophy of his day."[66]

Epicurus' school and teaching career. It was with and within this philosophical structure, which he constructed during the decade or so following his military service in Athens, that Epicurus began to gather and instruct students. He did so over the following half decade or so, teaching for a year in Mytilene, the chief city on the island of Lesbos, followed by a four-year stint in Lampsacus along the coast of the Hellespont (now called the Dardanelles), and finally in Athens, where he moved in 306 BC.

The move to Athens was, as Rist assures us, "an obvious move for two reasons." One, Epicurus "himself was an Athenian" citizen. Two, "Athens was the center of the philosophical world."[67] There is one other reason that is, perhaps, less obvious. This reason has to do with the turmoil that Epicurus had experienced in attempting to set up his school in Mytilene. In short, Mytilene was the sanctioned turf of the Aristotelians. And even though Epicurus had received the necessary signatures—as it were—to teach in the public spaces there, the Aristotelians seemed to have pushed for his removal. Consequently, he moved to Athens where he could acquire his own private property to set up his own school.

Epicurus called his property—a portion of it, anyway—the Garden (*Kēpos*). And so the name of his school. The Garden was a hierarchically run philosophical association where people—men and women, free and slave, Greek and non-Greek, as we have noted—could come to learn Epicurus' philosophy. More importantly, however, they could live the simple Epicurean lifestyle in friendship with others, a life that ideally bore the fruit of happiness.

Epicurus' remaining life and death. The truth is we do not know much about the details of Epicurus' life down to his death. We know he "sailed across the [Aegean] Sea to Ionia to visit his friends" in Lampsacus, and that he kept a fairly regular life in the Garden teaching and practicing the Epicurean way of life. "His friends came to him from all parts and lived with him in his Garden."[68] Otherwise, the sources remain mostly silent.

As for his death, his successor Hermarchus reports that Epicurus expired due "to stones that blocked the flow of his urine." He perished in a bath of warm water, comfortably numb, accompanied by a pitcher full of strong wine. Diogenes Laertius concludes that "Epicurus died in Athens in the second year of the 127th Olympiad, in the archonship of Pytharatus. He was seventy-two."[69] Depending on how you count, and on which scholar you consult, the year was 271 or 270 BC.[70]

Epicurus' writings. Diogenes Laertius reports that Epicurus "was a most prolific writer" who wrote "about three hundred rolls" that were full of his own words and ideas rather than "citation[s] from other authors."[71] These writings touched on all the major areas of ancient philosophy—on how we come to know reality (epistemology), on the nature of that reality (physics or natural philosophy), and on how we might live well within that reality (ethics). Of the three hundred rolls, Diogenes Laertius lists forty-one of what he terms "the best" of his writings. We still possess fragments of Epicurus' major work *On Nature*. Aside from bits and pieces, however, we have little of his larger works. Nothing remains, for example, of his *Teachings on the Feelings*, or of his *On Atoms and Void*, or of the four books of his *On Human Life*.

That said and properly lamented, Diogenes Laertius fortunately preserved four important summaries of Epicurus' teachings. Three of the four are in the form of letters—doubtlessly part of the "Letters of Epicurus" that he includes in his top forty-one best list. Two have to do with Epicurus' philosophy of nature and what we may call his general scientific or epistemic method. They are the *Letter to Herodotus* and the *Letter to Pythocles*. The other one, the *Letter to Menoeceus*, states Epicurus' basic ethical teachings, with an emphasis on how to live well and be happy. Otherwise, we possess Epicurus' *Principal Teachings* (*Kuriai Doxai*), a work that also made the top forty-one best list. Intended for memorization, the *Principal Teachings* are forty brief remarks about how to flourish. Similar to these is another collection of sayings known as the *Vatican Sayings*.

Ancient sources for Epicurus and Epicureanism. Aside from Epicurus' own writings and sporadic fragments found in ancient historians and essayists, early Church fathers, and a few others, there are only a handful of significant sources that help us understand what Epicurus was up to.

One of the most important is the first century BC Roman poet Lucretius. In his epic poem *On the Nature of Things* (*De Rerum Natura*), he sympathetically presents Epicurus' system and Epicurus himself as the liberator of humankind. Another is the slightly older Philodemus of Gadara, who was the "house philosopher of Julius Caesar's father-in-law, Calpurnius Piso Caesoninus."[72] Although much of Philodemus' work is in poor shape (it was discovered just two hundred fifty years ago beneath layers of volcanic ash in Herculaneum in Italy), books such as *On Anger*, *On Frank Speech*, and *On Death* nevertheless offer an invaluable picture of what it was like to practice Epicurus' philosophy. A third source is Philodemus' near-contemporary, the Roman statesman Cicero, who wrote about Epicurus' philosophy in several of his works. The most significant work for us, though, is his *On the Ends of Good Things and Bad Things*, in which he offers a dialogue between his Epicurean friend, Torquatus, and Cicero himself that explores the positive and negative aspects of Epicureanism.[73]

Moving into the present era and the time of the Roman Empire, other important sources include Seneca's letters to Lucilius and other writings (first century AD), several of Plutarch's essays (first and early second century AD), and, it almost goes without saying, the tenth and final book of Diogenes Laertius' third century AD *Lives and Sayings of Eminent Philosophers*, our most valuable source for Epicurus and Epicureanism.

The last significant ancient source comes from Diogenes Oenoanda (alternatively given as Oinoanda), an individual we know next to nothing about, aside from the fact that he must have been a wealthy man, who lived in the Roman province of Lycia, in what is now south-western Turkey.[74] On a wall that would have stretched as long as a soccer or football field, he left an inscription setting out the Epicurean path to understanding and happiness. Unfortunately, we only possess 223 fragments of the inscription. Nevertheless, they shed much light on Epicureanism that we would not otherwise have, meriting Diogenes Oenoanda our gratitude.

THE BIG THEMES & IDEAS OF EPICURUS & THE EPICUREAN WAY

The goal (telos) or good (agathos) of life—happiness and the nature of Epicurean happiness. Diogenes Laertius reports that Epicurus wrote a work called *On the Goal of Human Life*.[75] Although we no longer possess it, we can guess its likely contents given what Epicurus elsewhere declares about the end or goal of human life.

First, he proposed that there actually is a "natural" goal (*telos*) of human life.[76] This means that Epicurus was no ancient existentialist out to freely determine his own essence in the face of an absurd cosmos. In this way, he was no modern. While he strongly believed in human freedom, he nevertheless held that the goal of life was something furnished by nature (*physis*). Consequently, it is up to human beings to discover and consider this goal that is, as one translation puts it, "fixed by nature."[77]

Having established the basic fact of a natural goal, Epicurus likely went on to define its general nature in terms similar to those used by Aristotle. In his *Nicomachean Ethics*, Aristotle suggests that the goal (*telos*) or good (*agathos*) of life "is the end for which men do whatever they do."[78] Along with Aristotle, Epicurus believed that this goal was happiness (*eudaimonia*), or blessed happiness, the state of being blessed (*makarios*). Simply stated, then, Epicureanism is the "practice [of] those things that produce happiness" since happiness is, as Epicurus said, "everything"—which is to say the goal of life.[79]

In itself, this was nothing new. Some form of happiness is the common goal found in most of Greek literature and philosophy going back to Homer.[80] It was his spin on happiness, however, that was, perhaps, something new.

Positively stated, to be happy is for Epicurus "to do well (*eu prattein*)."[81] Said another way, happiness is a kind of overall health, what he calls "true health."[82] This "true health" consists of a healthy body and a healthy soul or mind. "The goal of a blessedly happy life," he declares, "is to secure bodily health and mental tranquility."[83] But when we begin to explore what this happy life or health is for Epicurus, we mostly come up with what it is *not* rather than what it is, a kind of apophatic approach to happiness.

According to Epicurus, happiness is more of an absence than a presence. Happiness is the absence of various negatives. "Everything we do," he says, "is for the sake of being free from pain and from fear. The soul's storm scatters as soon as we achieve this condition. Then we have no need to go around looking for anything that is lacking or seeking something else by which the good of the soul and of the body will be fulfilled."[84] From this we see that happiness—or the good of the soul and the body—is tantamount to the absence of something, in this case, the absence of a storm.

Epicurus used several terms to describe this condition of absence. Regarding the body, he stated that the goal is to be "free from disturbance (*aochlēsia*)."[85] As for the soul, he used three terms. One describes an undisturbed (*athorubos*) state of mind. As he put it in the *Letter to Pythocles*, "We have come to the point where our life has no need for non-rational and empty opinion. Our one need is to live undisturbed, without trouble (*athorubos*)" —that is, untroubled in mind by the thoughts and feelings that may arise from groundless views. Another term designates the experience of calmness or a calming (*galēnismos*).[86] This state of mind is the calm after the storm, the absence of excitement or agitation of various forms. It is here that we can imagine the peaceful, clear blue sea of Epicurus' childhood—the sea after a great storm has passed. Finally, the catchall term used by Epicurus is *ataraxia*. Defined for what it negates, *ataraxia* is a lack of trouble, disorder, and confusion in the mind. Stated in positive terms, it is calmness, tranquility.

Given what we've learned about Epicurus' understanding of happiness, that it is more an absence than a presence, it may be surprising that he emphatically declared that "pleasure is the beginning point and goal (*telos*) of living happily." After all, isn't pleasure something positive?—a present rather than an absent phenomenon? Certainly that is what much of modern epicureanism and the present-day epicure is all about. Even so, apparently it was not the case for Epicurus. For him pleasure was also an absence. In the *Letter to Menoeceus*, Epicurus explains that by pleasure,

> we do not mean the pleasures of decadent men or the pleasures of sensuality, as some ignorant persons believe, or those who do not agree with us, or those who have willfully misrepresented our position. Rather, by pleasure we mean *the absence* of pain in the body and of trouble in the soul.[87]

Obstacles to reaching the goal. If happiness in terms of a condition of absence, or of "pleasure," or of "bodily health and mental tranquility" is the goal of human life, then what obstacles prevent us from reaching the goal?

According to Epicurus, there are several underlying reasons that explain why we are oftentimes unhappy or disturbed. First, there is what we think we know about the nature of things—both things objectively and subjectively. The truth is our so-called knowledge is oftentimes actually a species of ignorance. We don't really know the nature of reality, nor do we know how to approach obtaining such a knowledge.

Consequently, this ignorance gives rise to a variety of disordered thoughts and disturbing feelings—confusion, despair, insecurity, and, most dreadfully, fear and anxiety. To mention just a handful of our concerns, both ours and those of men and women in the ancient world, we're afraid of the gods, of the future, of dying, of life after death, of lightning flashing across the sky and the earth shaking beneath our feet, of others harming us, and of whether or not we'll be able to secure what it takes to live. These thoughts and feelings are the second obstacle to reaching the goal of life. It is hard for tranquility to exist amid a storm of dread and anxiety.

Speaking of the storm, third, there is desire (*epithumia*). More specifically, there are certain kinds of desire that cause us to seek pleasures that are always mixed with pain. The problem once again is really one of ignorance. We don't know which desires to satisfy and which ones to leave alone. Accordingly, we end up feeding the fires of desire that need not be fed and tend to burn us rather than letting them die out.

Finally, there's the fact that we haven't chosen to be happy. Not really, anyway. And so we haven't practiced what it takes to be happily tranquil.

In sum, aside from the usual effects of the human condition, effects we can easily live with if necessary, the significant obstacles to happiness are ignorance, negative thoughts and emotions, certain kinds of desire, and the fact that we haven't truly chosen and practiced happiness.

The three parts of Epicurus' system. Given the fact of obstacles blocking the way to happiness, the most significant question becomes this: how can we overcome these obstacles? The answer is Epicurus' general philosophical system—his canonics, physics, and ethics. Here's how Diogenes Laertius summarizes the three:

> [Epicurus] divides philosophy into three parts—the canonical, the physical, and the ethical, which is to say canonics, physics, and ethics. . . . The

canonical part deals with the standard or criterion of truth, that is, the means by which one may judge what is true. It also deals with the first principle, or the elementary part, of philosophy. The physical part is about becoming and perishing, as well as other aspects of nature. The ethical part, on the other hand, considers human life, that is, what is best to choose and what is best to avoid, as well as the end or goal of human life.[88]

Let's look at each of the parts of Epicurus' philosophy in turn. In doing so, we'll learn how best to overcome the obstacles to reaching the goal of human life and how to choose and practice happiness.

Canonics. Know well what you know—and leave the rest alone.[89] Before moving on to investigate how we may know with confidence, we would first do well to summarize how it is that we—or rather the typical man or woman Epicurus would have been addressing— understand things, and what kinds of thoughts and feelings such knowledge generates. Aside from our own direct experience of life, which is often frightening, we resort to a variety of authorities that assist us in knowing the nature of reality and ourselves. Most importantly, there are the myths we've been told from the very beginning of our lives, the explanatory stories found in Homer, Hesiod, and others. Secondly, there are the fortune tellers, as Epicurus' own mother apparently was, and the diviners and oracle mongers, who interpret various mysterious signs to us and tell us about the future. Lastly, there is the speculation of the natural philosophers, including the "astrologers" or "astronomers," who tell us about the spectacles in the sky and how such phenomena influence us.

Epicurus would caution us against each of these sources of purported knowledge. As for the first, he states that "the exclusion of myth [in understanding nature] is the sole condition necessary." Again: "It is impossible to set ourselves free from fear regarding the most important things if we do not understand the nature of the whole cosmos, and if we are apprehensive about what the myths tell us." The problem is not the stories themselves but the fear and other negative feelings that arise because of the stories. Then again, the natural philosophers and their theories may make us feel even worse. For example, regarding a kind of determinism or destiny proposed by these thinkers, Epicurus declares, "It would be better . . . to accept the myths told about the gods than to bow beneath the yoke of destiny that the natural philosophers have imposed." As for the diviners and their ilk, Diogenes Laertius explains that "Epicurus rejects everything having to do with prophecy and divination" because it impinges upon our sense of freedom and control. If the future is set so that it may be read and predicted, then we are not free and have no control over our lives.

The underlying problem with each of these sources of knowledge is two-fold. One, even though they parade themselves as certain and authoritative, they are not. Two, such unfounded knowledge leads to negative feelings and a life that is less than at peace or happy. The question for Epicurus, then, was similarly two-fold. One, what knowledge *is* authoritative? And two, how should we expect to think and feel as a result of such knowledge? This is where we truly get to his canonics.

Epicurus posited that in order to consider anything regarding the world around us, we must first reflect on and be confident in how it is we know anything at all. Such consideration will yield an epistemic yardstick—a measure or rule or canon (*kanōn*, hence, canonics), by which we are able to know what is real. As such, Epicurus proposed his canonics as the general remedy for human ignorance.

Does this mean that Epicurus found the doorway to everything knowable? Not at all. But for him, knowledge about everything is unnecessary. Instead, a limited, well-conceived doorway to knowledge is large enough to enter the room where a certain measure of confidence exists that will allow us to choose and practice happiness, the goal of life.

The latter point is essential to understanding what Epicurus was all about. In his own words:

> We must hold that the function of the study [or knowledge] of natural phenomena is to clearly understand the cause of the most important things. And we must hold that blessed happiness depends on this.

And:

> In the first place, remember that, like everything else, knowledge of celestial phenomena—whether taken along with other things or in isolation—has no other purpose than tranquility of mind and resolute conviction and confidence.[90]

What we want is a measure of confidence about what is real, what is true. The goal of epistemology, therefore, and thus canonics, is to get at reality or the truth of what is real. But again, it bears repeating: we are not pursuing what is real in an absolute or unrestricted sense but only in relation to "the most important things," or those things that help along our practice of happiness. As for what remains—well, we will see how Epicurus deals with other non-essential phenomena as we go along.

Reality and its relation to knowing.[91] For Epicurus, reality has two basic components. First, there is that which sets things in motion or produces real effects. In his own words, "Things that are not real do not produce real effects,"—or, to give an alternative translation, "Things that are not do not move things." To state it in positive terms, things that *are* real *do* produce real effects or set real things in motion. The idea seems to be that there can be no motion without a mover, or no effect without a cause. Consequently, if there *is* motion or an effect, then there *is* a mover or a cause. The motion itself or the effect itself is the other component of reality. In conclusion, both the thing that is moved (the motion) or caused (the effect) and the thing that is the mover or the cause are the real things that Epicurus' epistemology is trying to reveal or uncover.

How, then, do we approach reality? Epicurus himself proposed three criteria of reality or truth, the means by which we are able to judge what is real and not real, true and not true. Diogenes Laertius reports that, "Epicurus affirms in *The Canon* that our sensations, preconceptions, and feelings are the criteria of truth." He goes on to state that later Epicureans "also generally include apprehensions or perceptions of mental presentations." Let's look at each of these criteria of reality-truth in turn.

Sensations.[92] We can safely affirm that for Epicurus, sensation (*aisthēsis*) included what we would call the five senses of seeing, hearing, smelling, tasting, and touching. Epicurus discusses seeing at length in the *Letter to Herodotus*, as well as giving a much briefer explanation of hearing and smelling.

In Benjamin Farrington's words, sensations are according to Epicurus "the impressions made on our sense organs by external phenomena."[93] In terms of the brief analysis of reality given a moment ago, sensation is that which is caused, whereas things sensed cause sensation. As Diogenes Laertius explains it, "Sensations are not self-caused." According to Epicurus, sensations offer the one sensing, or the knower, direct and pure information about reality—pure in the sense that sensations do not "add to or take anything away from whatever it is that causes them." Does this mean that sensation offers an accurate image of reality? The simple answer is yes, if by accurate we mean simply how a thing appears, sounds, smells, etc., to the one sensing.

To give an example, when the sense of sight from one vantage point sees an oar in water, the oar appears bent.[94] Strictly speaking, the sense of sight is merely conveying the "image" or "presentation," what we may term the *sense information*, of the bent oar to the one sensing. If the one sensing were to dive beneath the water to see the oar from that vantage point, or pull the oar from the water, the oar would appear straight. Well, we may ask, which is correct? For Epicurus, the answer is both. As he puts it, "one sensation cannot refute another homogeneous sensation." To say it differently, in of itself, one seeing cannot disprove another seeing. Whether standing above the water or emerged below, the sense of sight accurately perceives the image thrown off by the oar in the water. The same may be said of the sense information given by a galloping horseman. The sound offers one impression or hearing as the horseman approaches, another just as he reaches us, and a third as he gallops into the distance (think of a police car or ambulance racing by, sirens blaring). In itself, each hearing is correct.

The key word in the example of the oar is *appearance*. In one case, the oar appears bent; in the other, the oar appears straight.

Appearance, however, is not the same thing as being, what a thing actually *is*.[95] We may wonder, then, what the value of sensation is if it merely offers the appearance (or the seeming sound, smell, etc.) of what a thing is rather than its being or actuality. For Epicurus, the answer is that "reason is wholly dependent on sensations," even though, paradoxically, "every sensation is devoid of reason." Without the initial sense information presented by sensation, reason has nothing to work with to judge or opine what is actually real instead of what merely appears real. But before we get to opinion, or the judgment of reason, we must look at the other two criteria of truth mentioned by Epicurus in *The Canon*.

Preconceptions.[96] A preconception (*prolēpsis*) is the notion or conception we have of a thing that originates with our general and ongoing experience or sensation of that thing. "The preconception itself arises from sensations." Diogenes Laertius explains that "by the term preconception, Epicureans mean a sort of apprehension, or a right opinion or notion, or a universal idea stored in the mind." A preconception, therefore, is the recognition of a category or type. "For example," Diogenes Laertius explains, "pointing at something, someone might say, 'Such is a human being.' As soon as the term 'human being' is uttered, we have the direct notion of a typical human being by means of preconception."

The same may be said of an oar. Assuming we are familiar with oars (as Epicurus must have been given his military training and service), when someone says "oar," we have the direct notion of a typical oar in mind, including the point that oars are straight. It is not so much that at that moment we analyze the nature of an oar, its parts and so on. That's not how we know that oars are straight. Rather, thanks to our repeated sensation of and therefore ongoing experience and memory of many oars, we simply have a direct, straightforward notion or preconception of what an oar is. "A preconception is the recollection of a frequently appearing external object."

Preconceptions, therefore, are not about reason, which is to say the analysis or judgment of reason. On the contrary, preconceptions are prior to analysis or judgment. As said a moment ago, "the preconception itself arises from sensations."

Nevertheless, as "clear" notions arising from sensation, preconceptions are essential for what reason can do in order to analyze and make clear judgments. As Diogenes Laertes puts it, "Matters of judgment in which we form certain opinions or beliefs depend on something previously clear. Utilizing these clear preconceptions, we are able to answer questions such as, 'How do we know whether this thing is a human being?'" Or, we may ask, How do we know whether this thing is an oar?—or whether this thing is straight? The implication is that as soon as we begin to doubt preconceptions, which have a kind of self-evident clarity, even if not the clarity of analysis, we begin to stumble. So it is that we must rely on preconceptions, which offer us clear notions of things, just as the various sensations offer us direct information from or about things.

Feeling.[97] For Epicurus, humans are "living beings." This means that we are self-moving organisms. But how do we move? And toward what? What motivates us, whether in body or mind, to go in one direction and not another or toward one thing and not the other? The answer is Epicurus' last criterion of reality, feeling (*pathē* or *pathos*).

Diogenes Laertius recounts that "Epicureans say that there are two feelings in every living being. They are pleasure (*hēdonē*) and pain (*algēdōn*)." Analyzing each feeling, he declares that "pleasure is an appropriate feeling, natural" to every living being; by contrast, "pain is strange, unnatural." The significance of pleasure and pain for Epicurus is that these two are the means by which we choose or avoid, move toward or away from something. "It is by means of these two feelings that animals either choose or avoid something." In other words, if we truly and carefully pay attention to these feelings, we will know what to choose and what to avoid.

We will learn more about this kind of knowledge when we get to Epicurus' ethics. For now, let's briefly explore one last criterion hinted at by Epicurus and posited by later Epicureans before turning to the part reason plays in judging what reality is—or, at the very least, how we are able to have true opinions.

Apprehensions or perceptions of mental presentations. First off, it is important to acknowledge that this last criterion is not well-defined by Epicurus. Consequently, scholars approach it variously. Some fail to mention it at all or include it under the heading of "sensation." Others regard it as having a double function. Even so, there's one point that all scholars seem to agree on and highlight, a point that comes through clearly in Epicurus' own writings: this criterion has to do with our mind or the thoughts within our mind. The point is that the mind itself is a kind of sense; the mind itself senses things.

What is the mind able to sense? Its sensing ability is twofold. One, it senses or apprehends sensible presentations or images, that is, sense information presented by the other sensations to the mind. As such, these sensible presentations become mental presentations. In this way, we come to understand how the mind comes into contact with or apprehends the information obtained by sensation.

Two, the mind senses mental presentations or images that do not originate with the senses. An example of this is the mental image we have of the gods. We do not see the gods, nor do we sense them in any other way by means of the other organs of sense. Nevertheless, says Epicurus, "knowledge related to [the gods] is manifest."[98] How? This knowledge or mental image apparently comes from the gods themselves, seeping directly into what we may call our body-soul complex (which is a bodily reality), and so into our mind (also a bodily reality), where the "clear notion" of the gods shows up. The idea is that real things are constantly giving off various presentations (sight, sound, or smell presentations, etc.) that interact with our body-soul complex. The great majority of these zip past us without any effect. Some, however, penetrate us so that our minds grasp the presentation as a mental image or presentation.

Reason and judgment. Reason utilizes the criteria of reality (sensations, preconceptions, and feelings in the form of pleasure and pain) to make judgments about what is real and what we should actually choose or avoid rather than what merely appears to be real or what merely appears to be choiceworthy or worthy of avoidance. Epicurus generally calls such judgments "opinion." Opinions may be true or false. But how may we know?

Principles or methods of knowing.[99] Epicurus offers several principles or methods by which we may know whether our judgments or opinions are true or false. The major ones are offered in what follows.

Stick with the canon. First and foremost, we must stick with the basic criteria of reality-truth to know what is real. Without them—sensations, preconceptions, feelings—reason has nothing by which to make judgments and form opinions or to choose and avoid what affects us. As Epicurus makes the point in the *Letter to Herodotus*, "If you oppose all sensation, then you will have no means by which to judge even those sensations you declare false." Summarizing the principle of sticking with the canon, with the criteria, Epicurus counsels, "We must by all means stick to our sensations, that is, simply to the present impressions . . . and similarly to our actual feelings. This way we may have the means of determining that which needs confirmation and that which is obscure." Or, he declares, "Our sensations and feelings" provide "the surest grounds for confidence."

One last point. We may wonder whether we should stick with our own sensations, preconceptions, and feelings alone, or whether we should also take into consideration those of others. Epicurus seems to indicate both. "Therefore," he advises, "we must attend to present feelings and sense perceptions, whether those of mankind in general or those peculiar to the individual."

Move from the known to the unknown. Two, we can utilize what is known to us to understand or interpret what is unknown. "We should interpret things that are unclear to us by means of those things that are apparent [clear] to us." For instance, how can we possibly understand what goes on in the sky? Answer: we can look for possible explanations within our own experience. To give one example, Epicurus explains that "the moon may possibly shine by its own light." Or "it's just as possible," he says, "that it may get its light from the sun." Why or how does he offer these two different possible explanations? He does so given his experience of things, using what is known to him in order to understand what is unknown. "I say this because in our own experience we see many things that shine by their own light and many as well that shine by borrowed light."[100]

Stick with the facts. Be satisfied with multiple possible explanations. These different possible explanations originating in experience or what we know lead us to another method of knowing, or, most importantly, of being satisfied with what we may *actually* know, what Epicurus calls the "method of plural explanation."

Sitting outside in the dark of night, we may anxiously wonder how or why the stars move across the sky. Or walking home from our fields one afternoon under dark storm clouds, we may uneasily wonder what causes lightning to flash across the sky or thunder to sound. As for the former, says Epicurus, some "astronomers" tell us that the gods move the stars. As for the latter, we all *know* from myth that Zeus is responsible for lightning and thunder. But are these explanations true? Do they accord with the canon, the criteria of reality? Epicurus tells us that if we stick with the facts presented by the criteria of reality and argue from what is known to what is unknown, then we will inevitably arrive at a number of possible explanations for many phenomena. After giving several possible explanations for lightning, for instance, he states, "And so, it may easily be observed that the occurrence of lightning is possible in many other ways, just as long as we hold fast to facts and take a general view of what is analogous to them." The same is true for thunder: "There are in addition several other ways in which thunderbolts may possibly be produced."

Still, shouldn't we be dissatisfied or bothered by the fact that we don't have an answer?—that these many explanations vary one from another in possibly significant ways? And if we don't really know the exact answer, then isn't it possible that Zeus really does throw lightning (*at* us!) and Poseidon really does cause earthquakes (beneath *our* feet!)?

For Epicurus, the answer is no. Regarding the latter fear (that the gods may act in frightful ways that negatively influence every human being), Epicurus states that regarding our knowledge and explanation of things, "the exclusion of myth is the sole condition necessary. And myth will be excluded if one properly attends to the facts in order to draw inferences about what is obscure." For Epicurus, it is important to exclude myth because the various myths are not grounded upon the criteria of reality but arise from the imaginations of poets. Has anyone ever seen Zeus hurl a lightning bolt?

Has anyone ever seen the gods move the stars across the sky at night? And yet these views lead us to feel anxiety and fear! So, judges Epicurus, we are feeling disturbed for no reason at all.

The big question, then, is this: what are the facts? Do the facts clearly point to one explanation or to multiple possible explanations?

After explaining from experience the possibilities that the moon may shine "by its own light" or "by borrowed light," Epicurus argues that "none of the celestial phenomena stand in the way." In other words, no information arising from the canon bars the way of both explanations. He goes on: "The latter point is true as long as we always keep in mind the method of plural explanation and the several consistent assumptions and causes." Then he gets to the truly important point: we should keep the method of plural or multiple explanations in mind "instead of dwelling on what is inconsistent and giving these inconsistencies a false significance so that we always fall back, in one way or another, upon the single explanation."

Why should we do this? Because as good Epicureans (let's say) we wish to know and organize our lives around reality rather than unreality. Part of this reality is that we may not be able to know with precision what is real or unreal about many things—particularly those things that are at a distance from us (as are those things in the sky) or anything else we cannot closely examine. Nevertheless, observes Epicurus, humans tend to obsess; we tend to desire and so offer single explanations for such phenomena (so the gods). The problem with such explanations is not so much the explanation itself but the fact that it has no apparent relationship with the facts, and, most importantly, the disturbed feelings that may come with such explanations. This is ultimately what we wish to avoid. We want to know well in order to think and feel well:

> Nor can we make our treatment always as clear as when we discuss human life or explain the other questions regarding nature—for example, that the whole of being consists of bodies and intangible nature, or that the ultimate elements of things are indivisible, or any other proposition that admits only one explanation of the phenomena to be possible. But this is not the case

with things in the sky. As for their occurrence, celestial phenomena allow for more than one cause and a variety of accounts of their existence—none that contradict sensation. In the study of nature, we must not accept empty assumptions and arbitrary laws. Rather, we should follow the promptings of the phenomena, the facts themselves. We have come to the point where our life has no need for non-rational and empty opinion. Our one need is to live undisturbed, without trouble. As soon as we suitably understand what may be plausibly said of everything—if everything is explained by the method of plurality of causes in conformity with the facts—we will realize that all things go on in an unshakeable manner, consistent and reliable. But when we pick and choose among the causes, rejecting one that is equally consistent with the phenomena, we clearly fall away from the study of nature and tumble into myth."

By tumbling into myth, we tumble into uncertainty, confusion, and fear, as everything comes to "rest in the lap of the gods," as Homer would express it. This means that there's no actual order to reality, no real rhyme or reason; rather, everything happens according to the arbitrary will of the gods. Epicurus implies that experience belies this notion. Our senses tell us that things do go on in an ordinary, regular manner. We may not understand why, exactly, but if we stick with the canon, the criteria of reality, we can at least form the opinion that "things go on in an unshakeable manner, consistent and reliable." But how, we may wonder, can we know that our judgments or opinions are themselves reliable?

Submit all views to the ongoing tribunal of evidence. The method of confirmation and contradiction. We may know whether an opinion is true or false according to the method of confirmation and contradiction. This method submits opinions to the ongoing tribunal of evidence, that is, to the criteria of reality. Diogenes Laertes explains the method this way:

An opinion is true if the evidence confirms and does not contradict the opinion. On the other hand, it is false if the evidence does not confirm and instead contradicts the opinion. Therefore, [Epicureans] have introduced the expression, "That which awaits confirmation." So, for example, before declaring that an object in the distance is a tower, one should approach the object and learn what it looks like when near to it.[101]

Does the object in the distance send clear sense information to the one walking toward it? Yes. Might we form an opinion regarding what the object is? Sure. We might say, "That thing looks like a tower." The problem, however, is that the sense information, though clear for what it is, is not clear enough for us to judge with certainty that "That object is actually a tower." To make this judgment requires more evidence, another sensation. The latter comes as we approach the object. Closer now, we are in the position to judge or opine with certainty whether the object is actually a tower. If the evidence confirms the judgment, then the opinion that the distant object is a tower is true. If the evidence contradicts it, then it is false. It may be, after all, that the object in the distance turns out to be the towering stump of an old tree.

To give another example, there are the planets, or what Epicurus in Greek calls "the wandering stars." If we judge that these wandering stars actually move from one place to another, we may or may not be right. As Epicurus admits, "Regarding the wandering stars, the senses say yes." Nevertheless, he goes on, we "must wait for confirmation." Unfortunately, since we are not in the position to move closer to these wandering stars (unless we possess a telescope or spaceship), we may never know whether they actually move or if they only appear to move. But that's no problem. In that case we can utilize what we know based on the criteria of reality to offer many possible answers to the question of the wandering stars. In doing so, we'll rest content with the facts rather than asserting that the wandering stars must be alive or that some other living being is moving them—assertions that are satisfying in some ways but dissatisfying in others in that they cause fear in us that some living being is up in the sky looking down at us, controlling the stars and us.

The whole point is that we want to know what is real, the nature of things. Epicurus' canonics aids us in getting there and gives us the confidence to live in the assurance of what we know. As for the nature of things, it is to that we must next make our move.

Physics or natural philosophy—discovering the nature of things.[102] In describing the three parts of philosophy, Diogenes Laertius explains that for Epicurus, "the physical part is about becoming and perishing, as well as other aspects of nature." Epicurus himself asserts that his natural philosophy is about "the true story of the nature of things" that will help us understand that "all things go on in an unshakeable manner, consistent and reliable." This understanding in turn will, as we've already come to grasp, deliver a measure of peace if we're willing to stick with the facts. As Epicurus states it: "Without the study of nature, there is no enjoyment of pleasures unmixed with fear and worry." So then, what is the nature of things? What follows offers Epicurus' view on the matter.

Four initial points: nothing comes from nothing (no ex nihilo); nothing falls into non-existence (no ad nihilum); the sum of things is ongoing with no beginning; the sum of things is infinite.[103] To begin, we must start with four basic ideas or principles.

One, nothing comes into being or arises from nothing or from non-existence. To discuss it anachronistically for a moment, the point is nearly the opposite of the Christian doctrine that God created *ex nihilo*, "from nothing." Christians have historically wished to stress the fact that God, and God alone, is responsible for what exists (and thus all things are radically dependent on him). He did not create using preexisting matter, whether water, earth, or some other material. Moreover, God created moved by his own inscrutable wisdom and will. By contrast, Epicurus wished to stress the reverse, hoping to avoid such an apparently arbitrary (to him) cosmos.[104] Again: "we will realize that all things go on in an unshakeable manner, consistent and reliable." For Epicurus, therefore, the gods are not responsible for things. They don't mysteriously or magically (as it were) cause things to spring up from nothingness. Zeus doesn't rub his divine hands together and poof! there's a ready-to-throw lightning bolt. Nor do things just spontaneously arise. No, things come from previously existing things. Here's how Epicurus conveys the idea in the *Letter to Herodotus*: "To begin with, nothing comes into being out of what is non-existent. Otherwise, everything could come into being from everything, and there would be no need for any seeds."

The corollary point to nothing comes from nothing (no *ex nihilo*) is that nothing returns to or falls into nothingness or non-existence (for the sake of a parallel construct, we may say, no *ad nihilum*). For Epicurus, the reason is straightforward: "If that which disappears is so absolutely destroyed so that it ceases to exist, then everything would soon perish since the disappearing things would be dissolved into that which is non-existent."

So, we begin with two points: things (whatever exists) do not arise from non-existence (nothing *ex nihilo*), and things may not fall into non-existence (nothing *ad nihilum*). As for the third point, it simply teases out a conclusion that follows from these two: the sum of things is ongoing. "The sum total of things—which is to say, everything—was always the same as it is now, and such it will always remain." Why? If nothing radically new appears *ex nihilo*, and if nothing disappears *ad nihilum*, then what we are left with is whatever now exists. This is not to say that things do not over time appear differently. They do. But whatever things are in their most basic sense, they do not come into existence or go out of existence. Therefore, everything must go on in some basic sense that we will explore in a moment.

It follows from this ongoing duration of things that there is no beginning to the sum total of things. What exists (again, in its most basic sense) has always existed. Otherwise, the sum of things would have to have originally come from nothing.

The final point is that the sum of things is infinite. Epicurus argues for the idea this way: "The sum of things is infinite. For that which is finite has an extremity, and the extremity of anything is discernable only in comparison with something else. Since the sum of things has no discernable extremity, it has no limit. And since it has no limit, it must be unlimited or infinite."

What we have, then, is an infinite sum of things that has, in its most basic sense, always existed and will always exist just as it exists now. The next query must be, What is the nature of these things in their most basic sense?

Bodies and place; atoms and void.[105] Everything, whether on earth or in the sky or anywhere else, is made up of bodies and place, which is to say atoms and void. "The whole of being consists of bodies and intangible nature." Or: "the sum total of things consists of bodies (*sōma*) and void (*kenos*)."

Given Epicurean canonics, why must this be true? The argument is straightforward. One, we see and otherwise sense bodies. Two, we see and otherwise sense bodies move. Consequently, three, there must be something through which bodies move. This something is called "place" or "void" (literally "emptiness," what we would call space). Interestingly, we cannot sense the void. It is intangible—which in this case means more than it merely cannot be touched (as in the sense of touch). Rather, it cannot be touched or grasped by any sense whatsoever. Nevertheless, we indirectly know that it exists thanks to the fact that bodies move, and, therefore, that there must be something through which they move. Void, then, or the emptiness, is the place through which bodies move. As such, the void does nothing. It is simply the stage upon which everything is done. "The void itself is able neither to act nor be acted on, but it simply allows bodies to move through it."

By bodies, Epicurus means whole things or separate things rather than the accidents or properties of these things. Some bodies are composites, that is, they are composed of other bodies. Other bodies are those bodies or elements out of which composites are formed. These latter bodies or elements are bodily or corporeal realities that are unchangeable. Epicurus invites us to think of them as strong and enduring, solid and indestructible. Most importantly, he asserts that "the ultimate elements of things are indivisible." Literally, they cannot be cut. Accordingly, in Greek they are *atomos* (uncuttable); they are atoms.

How did Epicurus know that such atoms exist? Could he see them with his own eyes or sense them in any other way? Not at all. Even so, beginning with sensible things—composite bodies—and keeping in mind the fact that things in their most basic sense cannot fall into non-existence, he could reason toward the existence of atoms. Here's part of his argument:

> We must reject as impossible the unlimited cutting and division of a finite body into smaller and smaller parts. For to go down such a path would

result in reducing everything to nothing. In that case, we would be forced to admit that the existent things that make up compound bodies—which is to say, atoms—can be reduced to non-existence.

To finish the argument: there must, therefore, be things that are unable to be cut. These things are atoms or what we may call indivisibles or uncuttables.

What are atoms like? First, atoms do not have parts, an observation that follows from the fact that they are uncuttable. We cannot divide atoms into parts (even mentally) since atoms are indivisible. Second, atoms are full, meaning they have "no emptiness in them." Third, each atom has three qualities that do not change: size, weight, and shape. As for the latter, atoms "vary indefinitely in shape." As for size, however, there is no such indefinite variation. How does Epicurus know this? "If atoms came in all sizes," he says, "then we would have by now encountered an atom large enough to see. But we have never observed this—nor can we conceive how an atom could become visible."

Next, we may wonder what atoms do and how they behave. The most important point is that atoms are constantly moving: "Atoms are in continual motion through the ages." Atoms move with equal speed through the void at the speed of thought:

> Atoms necessarily move with equal speed when travelling through the void without meeting resistance. Heavy atoms will not travel quicker than small and light ones—assuming nothing encounters them. Nor will small atoms travel quicker than large ones if atoms find a passage suitable to their size, and if they are not obstructed in their movement. . . . As long as there is either motion, it must continue at a speed as fast as thought itself as long as there is no obstruction.[106]

Epicurus explains that, if not for other atoms, single atoms would travel indefinitely through the void. Since there are other atoms, however, they bounce or rebound off one another. When such a bounce occurs, one of two results may happen. One, the atom may rebound a long way from the atom against which it bounced. Otherwise, it may almost immediately bounce into another atom or a cluster of other atoms. If that happens, then the atom may oscillate, or bounce back and forth, between these atoms thanks to the void between the atoms, "imprisoned," as Epicurus says, "in a mass of entangling atoms."

Where do we stand so far? We stand amid an infinite sum of things that had no beginning and will have no end—atoms moving through the void and bouncing off one another.

We know these atoms end up forming composite bodies. But what sort of composite bodies or things are formed? On the large scale, there are whole worlds. Epicurus tells us that "a cosmos (*kosmos*), or a world, is a circumscribed portion of the sky, which contains stars, an earth, and all other visible things. It is cut off from the infinite, terminating in an exterior that may either revolve or be at rest." By cosmos he doesn't mean simply our own world alone; rather, Epicurus argues that "there is an infinite number of such worlds"—including worlds within worlds and worlds between worlds and worlds with varied shape, whether "round or triangular" or otherwise.

Considering our own world, everything within it was formed by atoms or the composite bodies formed by atoms.

> The sun and the moon and the remaining stars did not come into being independently from our world only later to be included in our world. Instead—like the earth and sea—they at once began to take form and grow by the accretions and whirling motions of certain substances of the finest texture, substances having either the nature of wind or fire, or of both. This, anyway, is what sensation suggests.

Even the gods are formed of atoms. But to them we will return in a moment when we get to Epicurus' ethics.

Next in our cosmos we come to us—to the ones who sense and form opinions. We too, says Epicurus, are composed of two basic bodily or corporeal realities, a body and a soul. These in turn are composed of atoms and void. The soul itself is composed of finer atoms or particles than those that make up the body. Epicurus explains that the soul is a bodily thing composed of fine particles dispersed throughout the whole assemblage of atoms in the human organism. The soul most nearly resembles wind with an admixture of heat. It is like wind in some ways and heat in others. But there is the third part that exceeds the other two in the fineness of its particles and thereby keeps in closer touch with the rest of the human organism. This is shown by the powers of the soul, its feelings, the ease with which it moves, its thought processes, and by all those things we lose when we die.

How do we know that the soul is a bodily or atomic reality? We do because incorporeal realities, such as the void, are "able neither to act nor be acted on." Therefore, as Epicurus argues, "if the soul were incorporeal, it would be able neither to act nor be acted on." But this is manifestly not the case, he concludes. It is the soul that is largely responsible for sensation, though the body or the rest of the human organism "provides the indispensable condition for the soul." It is the soul that feels and so moves us toward or away from things. It is the soul that thinks, that judges, that concludes and forms opinions. Most importantly, we clearly notice the soul's absence when someone dies. The body remains while that which animated the body vanishes.

Death, then, is the scattering of the soul. It is thus the loss of all sensation and all thought processes, something which is, to many of us, a frightening prospect. For Epicurus it was not. But to see why, we must move from his understanding of nature—this everlasting reality made up of atoms and the void—to his understanding of how we may live well given the time we have. For, as he states in the *Vatican Sayings* 14,

We come into being only once and will not be born a second time. Rather, we necessarily will never exist again—forever. And though you have no power over tomorrow, you put off feeling joy today. Life is consumed by such indecision and procrastination! And so, each one of us is dying without engaging in life today.

. . .

Ethics. According to Epicurus, the ethical part of philosophy answers an urgent question that every human being asks: how shall we best live? Diogenes Laertius explains that it "considers human life, that is, what is best to choose and what is best to avoid, as well as the end, or goal, of human life."[107]

Happiness. As for the goal, we've already seen that it is happiness understood as an absence: freedom from pain, from disturbance, from excitement or agitation, and from trouble, disorder, and confusion. Stated positively happiness is pleasure, health, and calmness or tranquility (which, in themselves, to reiterate, are conditions of absence).

A philosophy of choosing and doing.[108] It follows from this goal that "what is best to choose" is happiness and "what is best to avoid" is the opposite. Epicurus' philosophy, then, sets before us the imperative that we must actively choose the goal of life and do whatever it takes to achieve it, getting around whatever obstacles that block the way. Part of the achievement is found in the path of knowing well (canonics) and understanding the nature of reality (physics or natural philosophy)—understanding that "blessed happiness depends on this." For Epicurus, knowledge or theory is always oriented toward practice. We know in order to do and be well. His is an active philosophy, therefore, of choosing and doing. So, advises Epicurus in the *Letter to Menoeceus*, "We must practice those things that produce happiness since if happiness is present, we possess everything, and if it is not, we do everything to acquire it." He goes on to say, "Do and practice those things that I have continually recommended to you, taking them to be the basic elements of living well."

Freedom versus destiny.[109] We can only choose, do, and practice if we believe we are free to do so. In the ancient world, such a belief ran contrary to ideas spread by myth—ideas that asserted the domination of fate, chance or fortune, and necessity—and the notions of some of the "natural philosophers" that imposed "the yoke of destiny" on everything. By contrast, Epicurus argues that we should scorn "the notion of destiny that some introduce as the master of all things." Necessity "promotes irresponsibility," he says, whereas we should take responsibility for ourselves. As for chance or fortune, it "is unstable." The bottom line: "our own actions are free." Epicurus urges us on with the notion that "the wise man directly takes on chance, face to face." As for necessity, "it is something bad," he acknowledges, "but there is no necessity to live by means of necessity."

Limiting the emotions.[110] Believing that we are free, then, we must take action to actively limit the scope or reach of the emotions we experience. These emotions are "certain irrational tendencies" that are not based on the criteria of reality and the judgment of reason. In other words, Epicurus suggests that by letting our minds run away from the evidence, we come to fear one thing, feel anxiety about another, or experience despair relative to a third. The proper limitation of these emotions, by contrast, must be solidly based on the facts of a situation. Do the facts truly merit fear, anxiety, or despair? In the *Letter to Menoeceus*, Epicurus explores two situations in which and ways by which we may properly limit our fears. The two have to do with the gods and death.

Do not fear the gods.[111] For many, if not most, in the ancient world, the gods could be a source of anxiety and fear. How would ancient Greeks put it? "We fear the gods," they would say, "what they think of us, how they'll judge us, what they'll do to us. When we look at the stars in the sky and experience other natural phenomena, such as thunder and lightning, an earthquake, or a hair-trailed star (a comet) streaking across the dark expanse of night, we feel astonished and a bothersome sense of suspicion and anxiety as if something bad is going to happen to us or the ones we love. These mysterious spectacles make us fear the gods and worry about what they might do to us. And the feeling is not only for now, during this life. We also dread what the gods will do to us after we die and sink beneath the earth. We live in terror of the painful punishments they may impose on us, horrible ones we'll have to endure, such as those suffered by Tityus, Tantalus, and Sisyphus in Homer. Or the ones that Plato mentions in his dialogues. Or the ones found in the poet Orpheus and others."

Epicurus did not believe people had to feel this way if they only knew the true nature of the gods. And what is that? First, according to Epicurus, the gods *do* exist. "There are gods," he writes. "And knowledge related to them is manifest." The problem is that most people do not understand the true nature of the gods. Epicurus tells us that "the gods are not such as the many customarily believe since the many do not carefully guard and thus maintain a consistent view about the gods.... This is so because the assertions of the many about the gods are not true preconceptions but false assumptions."

In truth, the gods are fundamentally no different from human beings, at least in terms of their constituent nature. Rather, like everything else that exists, the gods are formed of atoms and void. Nevertheless, thanks to an ongoing renewal of their atoms, they are indestructible. Moreover, they are supremely happy, so much so that their happiness is of "the highest kind, . . . [and] cannot be increased." How does Epicurus know that the gods are, as he puts it, "blessed and indestructible"? He does because, as he notes, "this is the commonly held understanding of the god, the common epithet in writing." And he's right. From Homer on, the poets commonly refer to the gods as "blessed and immortal," which is to say indestructible.

What follows from the fact that the gods are blessed and indestructible? For Epicurus, the nature of the gods should determine what we should not or should say about the gods. As with anything else, conclusions should follow from facts.

> Accordingly, do not attribute to [the god] anything that is contrary to his indestructibility or incongruous with his blessed happiness. Instead, think about the god whatever can defend and uphold his blessed happiness and his indestructibility.

People like to think and say that the gods are busy running our world, steering the stars and other things in the sky. Or that the stars *are* gods. People imagine that the gods think about us all the time, planning our lives for better or worse, sometimes with delight and sometimes with anger. But this is not the case, and so we should not think it, says Epicurus. Rather, referring to such managerial business, he states that "a blessed and indestructible being is not bothered by troublesome business, nor does this being trouble others. Therefore, such a being is free from anger and the feeling that he is obliged to grant favors." Accordingly, in our conclusions about the gods, "the divine nature must be kept free from the task and in perfect bliss."

The argument may be summarized as follows: we should not fear the gods because they will never harm us. The gods will never harm us because they are too busy being perfectly happy to be at all concerned for us.

Do not fear death since death is nothing to us.[112] We are all familiar with Benjamin Franklin's remark that "in this world nothing can be said to be certain, except death and taxes." Death is a fact.[113] Epicurus poetically states that "each of us was poured a mortal mixture to drink at our birth." The unfortunate truth, however, is that this fact may give rise to certain feelings of insecurity. "We may possibly provide security against other dangers, but when it comes to death, we men all live in a city without walls." Epicurus realized that most people fear death. Consequently, most people experience considerable anxiety about death—about the pain that may come with it, or "we are in dread of the mere insensibility of death." So what, then, should we do about these feelings?

The imperative thought and practice relative to this fear and anxiety is that we "should get used to the idea that death means nothing to us," an attitude that follows from the nature of death itself. "Death means nothing to us," says Epicurus, "because the body, when it breaks up into its various elements, has no sensation. And that which has no sensation is nothing to us." Not only that but "life" by definition excludes "death" just as "death" excludes "life"; therefore, strictly speaking, death has no bearing upon the living (which is what we humans are). Here's how Epicurus puts the point:

> So then, death—that evil which most causes us to shudder—means nothing to us since when we exist, death is not present, and when death is present, we do not exist. In fact, death means nothing either to the living or to those who have finished living since it does not exist for the former, and the latter no longer exist.

Death is nothing to us, therefore, because, one, when we are dead we are not, and, two, when we are dead we do not feel—neither pleasure nor pain.

Someone may object, however, that he would prefer to go on feeling pleasure forever rather than feeling nothing at all. As a result, such a one pines for immortality. Epicurus counters that immortality is impossible for humans. We know this because we know that all human beings are mortal. Rather than looking upon this knowledge as depressing, however, Epicurus judges that it is a good thing for us. "It follows that a right understanding of the fact that death means nothing to us makes the mortal nature of life beneficial to us . . . by taking away the yearning for immortality." How does this "taking away the yearning for immortality" work? Something like this:[114] if one truly understands that immortality is impossible (which is, for Epicurus, a fact), then the irrational yearning for it will give way to a rational acceptance of *what is* for the one who wishes to base one's life on what reality *actually is*. Such a one will realize that pining for what is impossible merely brings dissatisfaction. Therefore, the practice of satisfaction demands that we not yearn for immortality.

How then should we face the uncertainty of the future (that includes our ceasing to exist) and the eventuality of death itself? Responding to these questions, Epicurus makes two key points. Regarding the future, we should neither presume its existence nor despair of its non-existence. "We should remember that the future is neither wholly ours nor wholly not ours. Accordingly, we must neither count on it as certain to come nor despair of it as certain not to come." And when we come to die, knowing that we have lived well, we should die well with non-attachment: "When it is time for us to go," says Epicurus, "we will depart from life, having no regard for it and for those who vainly cling to it, and proclaiming aloud in a beautiful song that we have lived well."

Pleasure, pain, and desire.[115] We noted above that, for Epicurus, happiness is pleasure (*hēdonē*): "pleasure is the beginning point and goal of living happily." Pain (*algēdōn*), by contrast, may serve to denote the unhappy life. Accordingly, we have two polar feelings: pleasure and pain. But what more can be said of them?

The point of the feelings of pleasure and pain is straightforward: they naturally serve to direct all animals toward or away from things. They are the means by which all "animals either choose or avoid something." Epicurus concluded that this bidirectional movement is entirely natural as demonstrated by how humans and other animals behave from the first moment of their birth. Diogenes Laertius reports that as evidence he "point[ed] to the fact that living things, as soon as they are born, are quite satisfied with pleasure, whereas they are naturally upset with pain—and this without rational reflection."

We may nevertheless ponder what exactly it is that does the moving. We may do so because pleasure seems to be more of a reward, the end goal, rather than that which moves or motivates us toward the end. It is what any animal naturally shoots for. That said, Epicurus never explicitly states what the actual mover is. In fact, he seems to identify it with pleasure, as pleasure is "the beginning point and goal of living happily," which we may interpret as meaning both that which moves us and that which is sought. Nevertheless, Epicurus does seem to imply that desire is the underlying motivating force. Desire moves us to seek things.[116] The problem with desire, though, is that it is not a clear-cut good like pleasure is. Rather, for Epicurus, desire has many faces.

According to Epicurus, we may categorize desire (*epithumia*), or the different kinds of desire, relative to whether they are natural or groundless, and whether their satisfaction is necessary or not.

> We must consider that of the desires, some are natural, and some are groundless. Of the natural desires, some are necessary, and some are merely natural. And of the necessary desires, some are necessary for happiness, some for freeing the body from disturbance, and some for living itself.

And:

> Of the desires, some are natural and necessary, whereas some are natural but unnecessary. Others are neither natural nor necessary but arise thanks to groundless notions.

Let's look at each kind of desire in turn, considering pleasure and pain as we go.

Natural and necessary desires.[117] Natural and necessary desires are those determined by human nature itself and its needs. As Epicurus counsels, "We must obey nature rather than doing violence to her. We will obey nature by satisfying the necessary desires and the natural desires, too, as long as they do no harm, but sharply rejecting the harmful desires." According to Epicurus, the three most significant needs or requirements of human nature seem to be "living itself" (survival), "freeing the body from disturbance" (such as hunger, thirst, and even disease), and "happiness" (health and tranquility).

These natural and necessary desires go after simple satisfactions rather than the kind pursued by other desires. Simple satisfaction is pleasure. In fact, even though Epicurus does not explicitly do so, we may confidently define Epicurean pleasure as "simple satisfaction." This is why Epicurus declares that "we have the need for pleasure only when we feel pain due to the absence of pleasure. When we feel no pain, however, there is no need for pleasure."

In this way, the absence of pain is the yardstick or the measure of the pleasure we require for happiness—for health and tranquility: "The standard measure for the greatest amount of pleasure is the removal of every pain. Whenever pleasure is present, as long as it lasts, there is neither pain nor distress nor both together." And: "We resort to pleasure when we use feeling as the measure for judging every good." Accordingly, if we imagine a sharp dividing line between pleasure and pain, pleasure is just *this side of* pain. Seen in this light, the following defense by Epicurus against some of his detractors makes perfect sense:

> When we say that pleasure is the beginning point and goal of life, we do not mean the pleasures of decadent men or the pleasures of sensuality, as some ignorant persons believe, or those who do not agree with us, or those who have willfully misrepresented our position. Rather, by pleasure we mean the absence of pain in the body and of trouble in the soul.

It is in this way—as the absence of pain—that pleasure is simple satisfaction (or simple satisfactions). "The flesh cries out, 'No hunger! No thirst! No freezing cold!' Whoever confidently has what it takes to satisfy these desires may rival even Zeus for happiness." We may announce our happiness as soon as hunger is satisfied. Or as soon as we are not thirsty. Or as soon as we are properly clothed, which is to say necessarily clothed. Diogenes Laertius recounts, "In his own letters, Epicurus declares that he was content with inexpensive bread and water alone." Here's what Epicurus says in the *Letter to Menoeceus*:

> Simple food gives just as much pleasure as rich food does as soon as the hunger pains are gone. A barley cake and water offer the highest possible pleasure when they are given to a hungry man. Getting used to simple and inexpensive food, therefore, aids the health of a man and enables him to perform the necessary requirements of life with resolution.

Natural and unnecessary desires.[118] The first point to note about these desires is that they are natural, which is to say they do actually correspond in some sense to human nature. The problem with them is that they demand and offer satisfactions beyond the needs or requirements of human nature. To give the example of one ancient commentator, simple water or an inexpensive wine both satisfy thirst. By contrast, costly, outstanding wines or ultrapure bottled water, we might say, are unnecessary. Why? Because we will experience no pain if we do not have them. "Unnecessary desires are those that lead to no pain if they remain unsatisfied. They involve an appetite that is easily relieved whenever its satisfaction is hard to procure or when it seems likely to cause harm."[119] The same may be said of sex. While the pleasure or satisfaction of sex is certainly natural, it is, strictly speaking, unnecessary to obtain or experience. "A man never gets any good from sexual pleasure; rather, he is content if he is not harmed."

Rather than pursuing simple satisfactions, natural and unnecessary desires seek a variety or diversity of satisfactions, things that are not necessary—again, strictly speaking—to support human nature and provision human needs. Given the dividing line separating pleasure and pain we imagined a moment ago (that pleasure is just *this side of* pain), these unnecessary desires drive us further into the realm of pleasure—that of complex and varied pleasures. "Pleasure in the flesh will not increase after need-based pain is removed. After that, pleasure may only be varied."

The same may be said about mental pleasure, though Epicurus does not directly make the point. While the very activity of doing philosophy brings pleasure ("in doing philosophy, delight coincides with the investigation"), there is a limit to what we should seek to know and therefore study. We study in order to understand just enough about the nature of things to avoid the fear and anxiety that may arise from ignorance (either the ignorance of simply not knowing or that of accepting false or unfounded conclusions). Epicurus asserts, "The function of the study of natural phenomena is to understand clearly the cause of the most important things," rather than, we might say, *all* things. He concludes, "We must hold that blessed happiness depends on this." Elsewhere he states that "knowledge of celestial phenomena . . . has no other purpose than tranquility of mind and resolute conviction and confidence."

What happens to us if we do not satisfy these unnecessary desires? Epicurus' answer: *nothing at all*. Again: "Unnecessary desires are those that lead to no pain if they remain unsatisfied." Rather, if we recognize them for what they are—unnecessary—they will simply vanish. On the other hand, if we continue to hang on to them, seeking their satisfaction as if such were necessary, then they will not vanish. "If one's zeal is intense in the case of those natural desires that lead to no pain if they remain unsatisfied, then such desires arise thanks to groundless notions. And when they do not vanish, it is not because of their own nature but thanks to those groundless human notions." This idea of "groundless human notions" leads us to the final category of desire.

Unnatural and groundless desires.[120] Unnatural and groundless desires are the product of faulty judgments. They are groundless or empty opinions about what human nature requires. We may earnestly believe we require more and more money or wealth. On the contrary, Epicurus responds, "Natural wealth is both limited and easy to get. But the wealth based on groundless opinion grows without limit." We may urgently feel that we need more and more food, not to mention a greater variety or complexity of dishes. Epicurus explains, however, that "the belly is not insatiable as the many declare. Instead, the opinion that the belly's satisfaction is without limits is false." (Note: Epicurus was no foodie; he was no modern epicurean.) When we have these kinds of desires, he says, we're just confused, mistaken about what we actually need:

> A pleasant life is not produced by stringing together one drinking party after another, or by having sex with young boys or women, or by enjoying fish and other delicacies set on a luxurious table. Instead, it is produced by sober reasoning that examines what is responsible for every choice and avoidance, and expels those beliefs by which the greatest confusion lays hold of the soul.

The point of understanding the desires: satisfaction, simplicity, self-sufficiency, happiness.[121] Stating what he does about the different desires, Epicurus concludes that such a knowledge (knowing which desires are natural, necessary, and grounded in knowledge versus groundless, unnecessary, and even unnatural) will help us to better choose and practice happiness:

> He who has a firm understanding of these things knows how to direct every choice and every avoidance toward securing bodily health and mental tranquility since this is the goal of a blessedly happy life. Everything we do is for the sake of being free from pain and from fear. The soul's storm scatters as soon as we achieve this condition. Then we have no need to go around looking for anything that is lacking or seeking something else by which the good of the soul and the good of the body will be fulfilled.

Epicurus' point is not that we should be a bore. Rather, his goal is to guarantee a life of ongoing satisfaction or a constant fulfillment. Such a life is accomplished by means of focusing on simple satisfactions rather than complex ones. It is the practice of simplicity that allows for a radical kind of self-sufficiency (*autarkeia*), which is, for

Epicurus, a state of affairs that is fundamentally valuable. "We regard self-sufficiency as a great good. This is not so that we may enjoy just a little in every case, but so that when things are scarce, we may nevertheless be satisfied with little."

The happy person is the one who is satisfied with *enough*—that is, with what human nature requires. The great news is that what is enough is easy to obtain. Epicurus tells us that "he who understands the limits of life knows how easy it is to procure what it takes to remove the pain of need and make the whole of life complete." He understands "that everything natural is easy to get, but whatever is groundless is hard." By contrast, unhappy (dissatisfied) persons are not satisfied with enough since they demand more and more. "Nothing is enough for someone for whom enough is very little." The problem is that this more and more is hard to get. But, says Epicurus, "there is no need for things that can only be procured by means of struggle and troublesome business."

One more point regarding simplicity and self-sufficiency. Epicurus argues that the person who is satisfied with little will actually enjoy plenty and variety more when they happen to appear (without any effort or trouble on his or her part) than the person who demands much and variety. Finishing his remark that self-sufficiency is "a great good," he states that the person who is "satisfied with little" is "genuinely persuaded that the ones who derive the greatest pleasure from luxury are the ones who need it the least."

A life of simplicity and self-sufficiency is accomplished by the judicial pursuit of pleasure, one that will often forgo some pleasures or endure some pains if such acts will result in greater overall or long-term pleasure. Epicurus expresses the point this way:

> Even though pleasure is our first and inborn good, we nevertheless do not choose every pleasure. Rather, we oftentimes forgo many pleasures when a greater annoyance will follow from choosing them. And oftentimes we acknowledge that many pains are better than many pleasures when an even greater pleasure follows from patiently enduring these pains for a long period of time. And so, even though every pleasure is naturally good and fitting, not every pleasure is to be chosen.

For Epicurus, the judicial pursuit of pleasure is a matter of judging how things will play out if one desire is satisfied versus another. He counsels that "We must present the following questions to all our desires. What will happen to me if the desire I wish to satisfy is fulfilled? What will happen if it is not?"

Whatever the answer to these questions, and however complex the calculus, the key thing to keep in mind is nature. "If at any moment you do not direct each of your actions to the goal of life indicated by nature, but, instead, you turn aside to some other goal in the act of pursuing some object [pleasure] or avoiding it [pain], your activity will not be consistent with the conclusions drawn from reason." What, then, does nature call for? If nature itself could act, what would nature do?

A hierarchy of pleasures. Aside from what we've observed above about natural and necessary desires, one last note on pleasure will help us to know what nature would seek in any given situation. Diogenes Laertius reports that Epicurus believed that "pleasures of the soul are greater than those of the body" just as "pains of the soul are worse" (than those of the body).[122] The imperative, then, is clear. In terms of need and therefore our attention and activity, soul pleasure takes precedence over bodily pleasure. This makes sense given the fact that Epicurus strongly emphasizes soul or mental tranquility (*ataraxia*). If we have that, the body's needs are very small indeed.

Practical wisdom and the virtues.[123] When Epicurus mentions "conclusions drawn from reason" or "judgment," he's really talking about what the Greeks and he himself called "practical wisdom." Practical wisdom (*phronēsis*), he declares, is "the greatest good." It is "the foundation of all these things" —that is, the means by which we may judiciously choose pleasure and avoid pain.

Yet more. Practical wisdom is essential because it gives rise to every other virtue or excellence of life, which makes living happily or pleasantly possible. "Every other virtue (*aretē*) is produced from practical wisdom, teaching us that we cannot live pleasantly without living wisely, nobly, and justly—just as we cannot live wisely, nobly, and justly without living pleasantly." Again: "The virtues have become one with living pleasantly. Living pleasantly is inseparable from the virtues." Epicurus offers the example of the just man who has peace of mind in contrast with the unjust man who is greatly troubled.

Nevertheless, virtue, despite its significance, is not an end in itself as it is in other ancient Greek philosophies of life. Instead, it is a means to an end. According to Diogenes Laertius' telling, Epicureans "choose the virtues for the sake of pleasure and not on their own account, even as we take medicine for the sake of health."

Friendship, the social covenant, and justice.[124] Aside from the virtues, wisdom also points us in the direction of others and friendship. "Of all the means that are procured by wisdom to ensure blessed happiness throughout the whole of life, by far the most important is the acquisition of friendship." And: "Friendship dances around the world of men calling out to all of us, 'Rise up to happiness!'" Why is friendship such a wise move and so happy-making? The answer is two-fold. One, there is the delight that arises from interacting with friends. The other reason, however, is even more essential. Friendship is one of the most important ways to have a sense of "personal safety" and "confidence," both of which are key components to a tranquil life.

Related to friendship on a larger social level is the compact (contract or covenant) that humans make with one another when they come together. The basic understanding of the compact is that they will not harm one another. For Epicurus, this is justice. "Natural justice is a pledge of reciprocal advantage neither to harm one another nor to be harmed."

According to Diogenes Laertius, Epicurus himself cared about and was a good friend to others. "There is an abundance of witnesses who attest to his unsurpassed goodwill and kindness to all men." Consequently, he had many friends, so many, Diogenes Laertius reports—though not without exaggeration—"that they could hardly be measured by whole cities." We see an instance of this friendship in what Epicurus writes to Pythocles: "In your letter that Cleon brought to me, you continue to show me an affection that matches my own devotion to you." So it was that he practiced what he preached.

LET'S GO!

As we have seen, Epicurus' philosophy was not merely about knowing how we know (his canonics) or knowing the nature of things (his natural philosophy). Instead, it was clearly aimed at acting toward the end of happiness (his ethics). For Epicurus, knowing was always pointed at doing; theory was always oriented to practice. As such we must keep in mind his all-important counsel to Menoeceus:

> We must practice those things that produce happiness since if happiness is present, we possess everything, and if it is not, we do everything to acquire it. Do and practice those things that I have continually recommended to you, taking them to be the basic elements of living well.[125]

The Classics Cave invites you to step into Epicurus' Garden. Come listen to Epicurus. Train in the good life with all his students and friends. Discover how knowledge is best founded upon the senses, preconceptions, and the feelings of pleasure and pain that naturally indicate what we should choose and what we should avoid. Explore the infinite nature of reality composed of atoms and void—a reality that had no beginning and will have no end. And lastly, practice happiness and those things that give rise to happiness.

As for the latter, you may wish to turn to Part 6, "Points of Wisdom & Ways of Practice." There you will discover "A Plan of Life Following the Philosophy of Epicurus," a twelve-point list of what may be considered some of the chief practices of living a truly Epicurean life. There are also Epicurean points of wisdom, as well as three workbook and journal-like prompts and exercises intended to motivate the reader to act toward happiness like a true Epicurean.

Whatever you do, be prepared to act, knowing that if you think and act well, you will be well—you will be satisfied, happy, tranquil. That, at least, is what Epicurus promises.

Note: As you read along, observe that you will always know where you are in The Classics Cave's *The Best of Epicurus* in a few ways. First, the very top of the righthand page will let you know what chapter you are in, along with the chapter's title—say, (Chapter) THREE ▪ ON NATURE: THE LETTER TO HERODOTUS. By the way, you should be aware that the chapter divisions and titles do not hail from the ancient world. Instead, they are provided by The Classics Cave to facilitate the reading and understanding of Diogenes Laertius' presentation of Epicurus in Book 10 of his *Lives*. You should also be aware that The Classics Cave has organized the material from Diogenes Laertius in such a way that should, again, make easier your approach to Epicurus, his life, and his thought. Rather than presenting it from beginning to end, we've moved it around some. That said, you will always know where you are in Diogenes Laertius' *Lives* by means of the bracketed numbers found in the text, such as [35], the numbered section that begins this book's (Chapter) Three. The *Principal Teachings* are part of Diogenes Laertius; therefore, you will find bracketed numbers as well as the number of each teaching. For example, "[143] 12" refers to Principal Teaching 12 found in section 143 of Book 10 of Diogenes Laertius' *Lives*. By contrast, the *Vatican Sayings* are not found in the *Lives*, and so there are no bracketed numbers given for them. Enjoy!

NOTES

[1] Athenaeus of Naucratis, *Deipnosophists* 8.25. The following passages from the same author and work are, in order, 7.8, 7.53, 3.77, 1.9, and 12.7.

[2] Homer, *Odyssey* 9.5-10.

[3] Athenaeus of Naucratis, *Deipnosophists* 12.67. The Christian father Basil of Caesarea had this sort of epicureanism in mind when he advised that "we must minister to the belly with what is necessary—but not with pleasant foods, necessarily, those delicacies sought after by those who look everywhere for table servants and cooks, scouring every land and sea, like those hauling tribute to a harsh master. This is a deplorable business in which one suffers things that are as unbearable as the punishments of Hades, where the inhabitants are forced to card wool into a fire or fetch water in a sieve and pour it into a perforated jar, experiencing never-ending suffering and toil." See *How to Benefit from Reading Greek Literature* 9.2 in *The Best of Basil the Great on Reading Literature and Education* (Sugar Land: The Classics Cave, 2020).

[4] Dane Gordon, "The Philosophy of Epicurus: Is It an Option for Today?", in *Epicurus: His Continuing Influence and Contemporary Relevance*, ed. Dane R. Gordon & David B. Suits (Rochester: Rochester Institute of Technology, Cary Graphic Arts Press, 2003), 9.

[5] Frederick Copleston, *Greece and Rome: From the Pre-Socratics to Plotinus*, vol. 1, *A History of Philosophy* (Westminster: Newman Press, 1946), 408.

[6] For Marcus Aurelius' path and the endowment, see Frank McLynn, *Marcus Aurelius: A Life* (Cambridge: Da Capo Press, 2009), 383-399, and E. Zeller, *A History of Eclecticism in Greek Philosophy* (London: Longmans, Green, and Co., 1883), 191-193. The four schools were the Academy or the Platonist school, the Peripatetic or the Aristotelian school, the Stoic school, and the Epicurean school.

[7] Diogenes Laertius, *Lives and Opinions of Eminent Philosophers* 10.9 (from here forward, *Lives*).

[8] Cited in Howard Jones, "Epicurus and Epicureanism," in *The Classical Tradition*, ed. Anthony Grafton, Glenn W. Most, and Salvatore Settis (Cambridge: The Belknap Press of Harvard University Press, 2010), 321.

[9] Dane Gordon, "The Philosophy of Epicurus: Is It an Option for Today?", in *Epicurus: His Continuing Influence and Contemporary Relevance*, 6.

[10] Howard Jones, "Epicurus and Epicureanism," in *The Classical Tradition*, 320.

[11] See Lucretius, *On the Nature of Things* 5.8-12.

[12] See Paul, Galatians 3.26-28.

[13] Diogenes Laertius, *Lives* 10.25, 28. See also Cicero's reference to the "bulky volumes to Themista" (*On the Ends of Good Things and Bad Things* 2.67).

[14] For the young, see Andre-Jean Festugiere, *Epicurus and His Gods* (Cambridge: Harvard University Press, 1956), 39.

[15] Diogenes Laertius, *Lives* 10.25.

[16] For John Locke, see Howard Jones, "Epicurus and Epicureanism," in *The Classical Tradition*, 323.

[17] Of course, Epicurus' own atomism was indebted to Democritus of Abdera and Leucippus. Not only that but various strands of Indian philosophy were developing similar atomist theories well before Epicurus. See Thomas McEvilley, *The Shape of Ancient Thought: Comparative Studies in Greek and Indian Philosophies* (New York: Allworth Press, 2002), 317-320.

[18] See Howard Jones, "Epicurus and Epicureanism," in *The Classical Tradition*, 322.

[19] Cited in James Warren, ed. *The Cambridge Companion to Epicureanism* (Cambridge: Cambridge University Press, 2009), 266-267.

[20] Pierre Hadot, *What is Ancient Philosophy?*, trans. Michael Chase (Cambridge: The Belknap Press of Harvard University Press, 2002).

[21] Diogenes Laertius, *Lives* 10.122, 85, 78.

[22] Anthony Gottlieb, *The Dream of Reason: A History of Western Philosophy from the Greeks to the Renaissance* (New York: W.W. Norton & Company, 2016), 318.

[23] Lucian of Samosata, *Alexander the False Prophet* 61.

[24] Lucretius, *On the Nature of Things* 5.8-12.

[25] Cicero, *On the Ends of Good Things and Bad Things* 1.14, 71.

[26] For Calpurnia and Plotina, see David Armstrong, "Philodemus, the Herculaneum Papyri, and the Therapy of Fear," in *Epicurus: His Continuing Influence and Contemporary Relevance*, 27.

[27] See "A Letter to Ambrogio Tignosi in Defense of Epicurus against the Stoics, Academics and Peripatetics," trans. Martin Davies, in Martin Davies, "Cosma Raimondi," in *Cambridge Translations of Renaissance Philosophical Texts*, vol. 1: *Moral Philosophy* (Cambridge: Cambridge University Press, 1997), 238 ff.

[28] See Howard Jones, "Epicurus and Epicureanism," in *The Classical Tradition*, 323.

[29] Ibid., 323.

[30] J.M. Rist, *Epicurus: An Introduction* (Cambridge: Cambridge University Press, 1972), ix.

[31] See Acts 17.16-21.

[32] Marianna Shakhnovich, "Theological Paradox in Epicurus," in *Epicurus: His Continuing Influence and Contemporary Relevance*, 158.

[33] Cicero, *On the Ends of Good Things and Bad Things* 2.31. As for "the swerve," Epicurus (as we know from Lucretius and Cicero) introduced it to explain, among other points, human free will. Rather than merely falling forever, downward and straight, atoms (somehow) minutely swerve so that they introduce indeterminacy into the sum total of things. Again, somehow this leads to human freedom, a reality which Epicurus insisted upon. See Lucretius, *On the Nature of Things* 2.218-220. For a full discussion of the swerve and its significance, see Stephen Greenblatt, *The Swerve: How the World Became Modern* (New York: W.W. Norton & Company), 187-189.

[34] Augustine, *City of God* 5.20.

[35] Lucian of Samosata, *Alexander the False Prophet* 47.

[36] See Lloyd P. Gerson, "Plotinus and Epicurean Epistemology," in *Epicurus: His Continuing Influence and Contemporary Relevance*, 69, 72, and 79.

[37] Augustine, *City of God* 8.7 and 8.5.

[38] A.E. Tayler, *Epicurus* (London: Constable & Company, 1911), 52.

[39] Augustine, *Confessions* 6.26.

[40] Dante, *Inferno* 10.13-15 (trans. Allen Mandelbaum).

[41] Clement of Alexandria, *Stromata* 2.4.

[42] Augustine, *City of God* 14.2.

[43] J.B. Pike, ed., *Frivolities of Courtiers and Footprints of Philosophers*, (Minneapolis: University of Minnesota Press, 1938), cited in Karen Bollermann and Cary Nederman, "John of Salisbury," in *The Stanford Encyclopedia of Philosophy*, https://secure.plato.stanford.edu/archives/fall2016/entries/john-salisbury/.

[44] John Stuart Mill, *Utilitarianism*, Ch. 2.

[45] Howard Jones, "Epicurus and Epicureanism," in *The Classical Tradition*, 323.

[46] Plutarch, *That It Is Not Possible to Live Pleasurably According to the Doctrine of Epicurus* 18.

[47] Diogenes Laertius, *Lives* 10.14.

[48] See Benjamin Farrington, *The Faith of Epicurus* (New York: Basic Books, 1967), 5 ff. for a good discussion, as well as Andre-Jean Festugiere, *Epicurus and His Gods*, 19-20.

[49] See, for instance, J.M. Rist, *Epicurus: An Introduction*, 3. The emphasis and thesis goes back at least to Eduard Zeller (1883).

[50] Diogenes Laertius, *Lives* 10.10.

[51] B. Farrington, *The Faith of Epicurus*, 5.

[52] For "schoolteacher" (*grammatodidaskalos*, sometimes given as schoolmaster), see Diskin Clay, "The Athenian Garden," in *The Cambridge Companion to Epicureanism*, 12. See also Diogenes Laertius, *Lives*, 10.3. For his mother's occupation, see J.M. Rist, *Epicurus: An Introduction*, 1.

[53] Diogenes Laertius, *Lives*, 10.2. Relative to this story, Sextus Empiricus (*Against the Physicists* 2.18-19) reports that when Epicurus' teachers told him that it was the business of philosophers to discuss such questions (i.e., the origin of chaos), Epicurus replied, "Well then, I must go to them, if they are the ones who know the truth of things that are."

[54] Hesiod, *Theogony* 116 from *The Best of Hesiod's* Theogony & Works and Days (Sugar Land: The Classics Cave, 2021).

[55] Diogenes Laertius offers both twelve (10.14) and fourteen (10.2) as the age of the initial contact and study.

[56] Diogenes Laertius, *Lives* 10.12.

[57] Ibid., *Lives* 10.14. See also J.M. Rist, *Epicurus: An Introduction*, 1, and B. Farrington, *The Faith of Epicurus*, 5.

[58] J.M. Rist, *Epicurus: An Introduction*, 2.

[59] Diogenes Laertius, *Lives* 10.13.

[60] See J.M. Rist, *Epicurus: An Introduction*, 2. Aristotle appeared pro-Macedonian as the former tutor of Alexander the Great, the king of Macedon.

[61] Such is Festugiere's conclusion. See Andre-Jean Festugiere, *Epicurus and His Gods*, 20.

[62] Though the significant point is *that* he did do so, there seems to be some controversy over when, exactly, Epicurus encountered Nausiphanes and studied with him. Rist suggests it was at some point during the ten years following 321 (see J.M. Rist, *Epicurus: An Introduction*, 3-4). Festugiere, however, declares that Epicurus studied with Nausiphanes when he was fourteen (see Andre-Jean Festugiere, *Epicurus and His Gods*, 19). For what Diogenes Laertius has to say regarding the matter, see *Lives* 10.2 (for Epicurus' move to Colophon and his study with other philosophers) and 10.13-14 (for the possibility of Epicurus'

being Nausiphanes' student, and what he possibly derived from him).

[63] Diogenes Laertius, *Lives*, 10.14.

[64] ". . . When [Epicurus] happened to encounter the works of Democritus, he took up philosophy." Ibid., 10.2.

[65] See Andre-Jean Festugiere, *Epicurus and His Gods*, 19, for a discussion of these terms and 23 (footnote 3) for a presentation of the Greek found in Diels-Kranz.

[66] B. Farrington, *The Faith of Epicurus*, 9.

[67] J.M. Rist, *Epicurus: An Introduction*, 9. For a similar conclusion, see B. Farrington *The Faith of Epicurus*, 11.

[68] For visiting his friends and for others visiting him, see Diogenes Laertius, *Lives* 10.10.

[69] Ibid., 10.15.

[70] Various authors give different dates. For example, A.A. Long (*Hellenistic Philosophy: Stoics, Epicureans, Sceptics*), J.M. Rist (*Epicurus: An Introduction*), and the editors of *Epicurus: His Continuing Influence and Contemporary Relevance*) give 271; Andre-Jean Festugiere (*Epicurus and His Gods*), Diskin Clay and Catherine Wilson (in *The Cambridge Companion to Epicureanism*), and the *Stanford Encyclopedia of Philosophy* give 270.

[71] Diogenes Laertius, *Lives* 10.26.

[72] David Armstrong, "Philodemus, the Herculaneum Papyri, and the Therapy of Fear," in *Epicurus: His Continuing Influence and Contemporary Relevance*, 20.

[73] We have included parts of this work in this volume. See Part 5, "Epicureanism as Presented by Cicero."

[74] See Michael Erler, "Epicureanism in the Roman Empire," in *The Cambridge Companion to Epicureanism*, 54 ff.

[75] Diogenes Laertius, *Lives* 10.30 and 136.

[76] See ibid., 10.133, where Epicurus contends that the better man "has considered the natural goal of life . . ."

[77] The translation is that of R.D. Hicks.

[78] Aristotle, *Nicomachean Ethics* 1.7.1.

[79] See Diogenes Laertius, *Lives* 10.122.

[80] For Homer's understanding of happiness, and a brief summary of what other Greeks thought, see Tim J. Young, *A Hero's Wish: What Homer Believed about Happiness and the Good Life* (Sugar Land: EuZōn Media, 2015). See also *Happiness: What the Ancient Greeks Thought and Said about Happiness* (Sugar Land: The Classics Cave, 2021).

[81] The point comes from Diogenes Laertius, who tells us that "in his letters [Epicurus] replaces the usual greeting, "May you be glad," with "May you do well" and "May you live earnestly." See Diogenes Laertius, *Lives* 10.14.

[82] *Vatican Sayings* 54: "We must not merely pretend to practice philosophy; rather, we must actually do it. For we do not merely need the appearance of health, but true health."

[83] Diogenes Laertius, *Lives* 10.128.

[84] Ibid., 10.128.

[85] See ibid., 10.127.

[86] *Galēnismos* comes from *galēnos* (calm), which oftentimes refers to the calm of the sea. It appears in Epicurus as *engalēnizō*, "to spend life calmly" (see ibid., 10.37), and *galēnismos*, "calming [of the mind]" (see ibid., 10.83).

[87] Ibid., 10.133. Italics added.

[88] Ibid., 10.29-30.

[89] For "*Canonics . . . ,*" see ibid., 10.78, 85, 104, 134-135, 143.

[90] We might also add, "Without the study of nature, there is no enjoyment of pleasures unmixed with fear and worry" (ibid., 10.143).

[91] For "*Reality . . . ,*" see ibid. 10.31-32.

[92] For "*Sensations,*" see ibid., 10.31-32.

[93] B. Farrington, *The Faith of Epicurus*, 108.

[94] Although Epicurus does not use this example, it is useful for us since we understand what is going on in terms of light, whereas Epicurus likely would have only had the barest grasp of some distortion.

[95] We must be careful here as Epicurus does not make an explicit distinction between appearance and actuality. Even so, it does seem to be what he is getting at, even if he does not believe we can get at the being of a thing.

[96] For "*Preconceptions,*" see ibid., 10.33.

[97] For "*Feeling,*" see ibid., 10.34.

[98] Ibid., 10.123.

[99] For the discussion of the various "*Principles or methods of knowing,*" see 10.32, 34, 38, 63, 82, 86-87, 94-95, 102, 104, 146.

[100] Think, for instance, of a candle shining in a dark room and the face of a friend that also shines, though with the borrowed light of the candle's flame.

[101] Regarding the origin of "falsehood," Epicurus states that "falsehood and error . . . are always based on judgment added to a presentation that awaits confirmation, or, at least, no contradiction." Further, he says that "error would not have occurred if we had not experienced some other movement in ourselves conjoined with, but distinct from, the apprehension or perception of what is presented. Falsehood results from this movement—if it is not confirmed or if it is contradicted. By contrast, if it is confirmed, or if it is not contradicted, then truth is the result" (Diogenes Laertius, *Lives* 10.50-51).

[102] For "*Physics or natural Philosophy,*" see ibid., 10.30, 85, 143.

[103] For the "*Four initial points . . . ,*" see ibid., 10.38-39, 44, 41.

[104] Arbitrary in the sense that the cosmos is based on God or gods who choose for whatever reason and by some inexplicable power to create rather than a cosmos based on always-existing things (atoms and the void) that necessarily form things, including whole worlds, when the atoms move through the void and become entangled.

[105] For "*Bodies and place; atoms and void,*" and related points, see ibid., 10.39-43, 56-57, 61, 63-64, 66-67, 86, 88-90. Sometimes Epicurus (or Diogenes Laertius) simply speaks of "void." Sometimes the definite article "the" is used, as in "the void."

[106] Compare an atom's speed to Homer's description of Hera's speed in the *Iliad*: she moved "as fast as the thoughts of a man" (*Iliad* 15.80).

[107] Diogenes Laertius, *Lives* 10.30.

[108] For "*A philosophy of choosing and doing,*" see ibid., 10.78, 122-123.

[109] For "*Freedom versus destiny,*" see ibid., 10.120, 133-135, and *Vatican Sayings* 9.

[110] For the general idea and method of limiting the emotions, see Diogenes Laertius, *Lives* 10.81-82. "Disturbances also arise thanks to the anticipation or suspicion of some everlasting evil—either because of the myths, or because we are in dread of the mere insensibility of death, as if it had to do with us. People are reduced to this state not because of conviction but because of a certain irrational tendency. Accordingly, if men do not *set limitations on their terror*, they must suffer as much or an even more intense anxiety than the man whose views on these matters are quite vague. But mental tranquility means being released from all these troubles and keeping in mind the general and most important points. Therefore, we must attend to present feelings and sensations, whether those of mankind in general or those peculiar to the individual. We must also attend to all the clear evidence available to us as given by each of the criteria. By paying attention to these, we will correctly and fully be able to explain the source of the disturbance and the fear, banishing it . . ."

[111] For the discussion of the gods and why we should not fear them ("*Do not fear the gods*"), see ibid., 10.77 (where Epicurus declares that the stars are "no more than globular masses of fire"), 97, 121, 123-124, 139. Further, we should "liberate the divine nature from troublesome duties" (see ibid., 10.113). In reference to the idea that animals indicate coming weather, Epicurus states that "no divine being sits observing when these animals go out and afterwards fulfilling the signs that the animals have given" (see ibid., 10.115).

[112] For the discussion of death and why we should not fear it ("*Do not fear death since death is nothing to us*"), see ibid., 10.31, 64-65, 81, 124-125, 127, 139, and *Vatican Sayings* 30 and 47. See Epicurus' brief *Letter to Idomeneus* as an example of how to die well (Diogenes Laertius, *Lives* 10.22).

[113] The fact was acknowledged from Homer on. For instance, in the *Odyssey* 3.236-238, the goddess Athena says to Telemachus, "Death that is common to

all men is certain. Not even the gods have the power to defend a loved man against it when the destructive fate of death finally drops a man to the dust." In the *Iliad* 18.117, 121, Achilles observes that, "not even was the mighty Heracles able to flee death." So, he says, "I will lay asleep when I die."

[114] "Something like this," because Epicurus does not explicitly work out the point.

[115] For *"Pleasure, pain, and desire,"* see ibid., 10.34, 127, 137, 149.

[116] We must be careful here not to read too much into Epicurus. An example may suffice to explain the difference between desire and pleasure. Thirst (the desire-for-water but also the pain, however slight, experienced simultaneously with or as the desire-for-water) motivates us to drink water to experience the quenching of thirst or the pleasure of non-thirst. Water (that which represents non-thirst, and so pleasure and the absence of pain) moves us from ahead. Desire-for-water (pain and so the absence of pleasure) moves us from behind.

[117] For *"Natural and necessary desires,"* see ibid., 10.11, 127 ("And of the necessary desires, some are necessary for happiness, some for freeing the body from disturbance, and some for living itself"), 128-131, 139, and *Vatican Sayings* 21 and 33.

[118] For *"Natural and unnecessary desires,"* see Diogenes Laertius, *Lives* 10.27, 78, 85, 148-149, and *Vatican Sayings* 51.

[119] There is a significant implied point here—that the "satisfaction" of any appetite should involve benefit rather than harm. Therefore, if satisfaction (pleasure) involves immediate or future harm ("when it seems likely to cause harm"), then one should avoid it. If it entails benefit, however, whether some present or future good, or if the result is neutral (one is merely "not harmed"), then one can choose it.

[120] For *"Unnatural and groundless desires,"* see Diogenes Laertius, *Lives* 10.32, 144, and *Vatican Sayings* 59.

[121] For *"The point of understanding the desires . . . ,"* see Diogenes Laertius, *Lives* 10.128-130, 144, 146, 148, and *Vatican Sayings* 68 and 71.

[122] Diogenes Laertius, *Lives* 10.137.

[123] For *"Practical wisdom and the virtues,"* see ibid., 10.132, 138, 144. To understand what the Greeks from Homer on thought and said about virtue or excellence (*aretē*), see *Aretē: Excellence or Virtue—What the Ancient Greeks Thought and Said about Aretē* (Sugar Land: The Classics Cave, 2021).

[124] For *"Friendship, the social covenant, and justice,"* see ibid., 10.9, 84, 148 (wisdom, here, is *sophia*), 150, *Principal Teachings* 31 (see also *Principal Teachings* 33: "Justice is an agreement neither to harm nor be harmed that is made when men gather together from time to time in various places"), and *Vatican Sayings* 52.

[125] Diogenes Laertius, *Lives* 10.122-123.

PART 1

CANONICS & PHYSICS
ON THE OBSERVATION & NATURE OF THINGS

EPICUREAN PHILOSOPHY
THE THREE BASIC PARTS & EPICURUS' WORKS

IN BRIEF: *Diogenes Laertius delineates and briefly describes the three basic areas of Epicurean philosophy—canonics, physics, and ethics. The chapter finishes with a list of some of Epicurus' works related to each part.*

I N WHAT COMES, I, Diogenes Laertius, will endeavor to give Epicurus' views that are expressed in his works. I will quote three of his letters in which he has given an epitome of his whole philosophical system. [29] I will also set down his *Principal Teachings* and any other of his views that seem worth citing. I will do this so that you may be in the position to study the philosopher from every angle and know how to judge him.

The first letter is addressed to Herodotus. It is about natural philosophy, or physics. The second letter is to Pythocles. It deals with things high in the sky, or celestial phenomena. The third letter is addressed to Menoeceus. It is about human life.

THE THREE BASIC PARTS OF PHILOSOPHY

We must begin with . . . some preliminary remarks about Epicurus' division of philosophy. He divides philosophy into three parts— the canonical, the physical, and the ethical, which is to say, canonics, physics, and ethics.

[30] The canonical serves as an introduction to Epicurus' system. It is contained in a single work of his titled *The Canon*. The physical part includes his entire theory of nature. It is covered in the thirty-seven books of his work *On Nature* and, in summary form, in his letters. The ethical part is about matters having to do with choice

and avoidance. It may be found in his work *On Human Life*, in his letters, and in his treatise *On the Goal of Human Life*.

Most people usually join the canonical part of Epicurus' philosophy with the physical part. The canonical part deals with the standard or criterion of truth, that is, the means by which one may judge what is true. It also deals with the first principle, or the elementary part, of philosophy. The physical part is about becoming and perishing, as well as other aspects of nature. The ethical part, on the other hand, considers human life, that is, what is best to choose and what is best to avoid, as well as the end or goal of human life.

[31] Epicurus and his followers reject dialectic, that is, the art of discussion, as superfluous. They hold that in their inquiries, natural philosophers should be content to employ the ordinary terms for things.

SELECTED WORKS OF EPICURUS HAVING TO DO WITH THE THREE PARTS OF PHILOSOPHY [27-28]

Canonics

On the Criterion, or *The Canon*
On Vision
On the Sense of Touch
Teachings on the Feelings—addressed to Timocrates
On Images
On Presentations

Physics

On Nature
On Atoms and Void
Epitome of Objections to the Natural Philosophers
On the Gods
On the Angle in the Atom
On Music

Teachings about Disease—addressed to Mithras

   Ethics

On Desire
Principal Teachings
On Choice and Avoidance
On the Goal of Human Life
On Piety
On Human Life—four books
On Just and Honest Dealing
On Fate
Discovery of the Future
Exhortation
On Justice and Other Virtues
On Gifts and Gratitude
On Kingship

CANONICS
THE CANONICAL PART OF EPICURUS' PHILOSOPHY

IN BRIEF: *Diogenes Laertius explores the three basic Epicurean criteria of truth—sensations, preconceptions, and feelings. Sensations serve as the foundation for all knowledge. Preconceptions generalize sensations, utilizing names or terms to denote what is meant by the preconception. Opinions are true or false depending on sensations. Lastly, feelings guide all living beings—animals—to choose or avoid various things.*

EPICURUS AFFIRMS IN *The Canon* that our sensations, preconceptions, and feelings are the criteria of truth. The Epicureans also generally include apprehensions or perceptions of mental presentations as a criterion. Epicurus' own statements regarding the canonical part are also found in the epitome addressed to Herodotus and in the *Principal Teachings*.

Sensation Epicurus says that every sensation is devoid of reason and incapable of memory. Sensations are not self-caused. Nor can sensations add to or take anything away from whatever it is that causes them.

Nothing can refute sensations or convict them of error. [32] One sensation cannot refute another homogeneous sensation, that is, one that is of the same kind or nature. Homogeneous sensations are equally valid. Neither can one sensation refute a heterogeneous sensation, that is, one that is not of the same kind or nature. This is so because the two kinds of sensation do not judge similar objects. (By the way, reason itself cannot refute sensations since reason is wholly dependent on sensations.) Since we humans equally pay attention to all sensations, one sensation cannot refute another. The reality of separate perceptions guarantees the truth of our sensations. Seeing and hearing are just as real as feeling pain.

It follows that we should interpret things that are unclear to us by means of those things that are apparent to us, that is, by various phenomena. This is so because all our notions arise from sensations either directly or, with the help of reason, they do so by analogy, resemblance, or combination.

Those things that appear to madmen and in dreams are real since they produce real effects. Things that are not real do not produce real effects.

Preconception [33] By the term preconception, Epicureans mean a sort of apprehension, or a right opinion or notion, or a universal idea stored in the mind. A preconception is the recollection of a frequently appearing external object. For example, pointing at something, someone might say, "Such is a human being." As soon as the term "human being" is uttered, we have the direct notion of a typical human being by means of preconception. The preconception itself arises from sensations.

For this reason, the preconception originally associated with every term is the right one, plain and clear. We would never begin an investigation, seeking something in particular, unless we first knew what it was we were searching for. For example, "The thing standing over there is a horse or a cow." Before knowing whether the thing is a horse or a cow, we must first know by means of preconception the shape or form of a horse or a cow. We would not have given anything a name, or assigned anything a term, if we had not first understood its general form by means of preconception. It follows, then, that preconceptions are clear. Moreover, matters of judgment in which we form certain opinions or beliefs depend on something previously clear. Utilizing these clear preconceptions, we can answer questions such as, "How do we know whether this thing is a human being?"

[34] Epicureans also call opinion "assumption." They say that opinions can either be true or false. An opinion is true if the evidence confirms and does not contradict it. On the other hand, an

opinion is false if the evidence does not confirm and instead contradicts it. Therefore, they have introduced the expression, "That which awaits confirmation." So, for example, before declaring that an object in the distance is a tower, one should approach the object and learn what it looks like when near to it.

Feeling Epicureans say that there are two feelings in every living being. They are pleasure and pain. They further say that pleasure is an appropriate feeling, natural. By contrast, pain is strange, unnatural. It is by means of these two feelings that animals either choose or avoid something.

Other There are two kinds of inquiry. One has to do with actual things, the other with words alone.

So much, then, for the basic division of Epicurus' philosophy, as well as the criterion of truth. We must now turn to one of the letters.

ON NATURE
THE LETTER TO HERODOTUS

IN BRIEF: *Epicurus first explains the purpose of the letter, which is to provide a general survey of his conclusions regarding the nature of things. He then reminds Herodotus to rely on clear terms and the criteria of sensation and feelings before moving on to a brief exposition of the nature of the cosmos, or world, as well as the likelihood of an infinite number of worlds. Everlasting and infinite, the cosmos has two basic elements, atoms and (the) void. Epicurus next explores the nature of seeing, hearing, and smelling, three ways by which we sense reality. He then discusses the properties, parts, and motion of atoms before exploring the corporeal nature of the soul and the significant role it has in sensation. Next, he explains what we sense in terms of properties and accidents, adding on a short reflection on how we should think of and speak about time. Moving on, he addresses the rise of multiple worlds from the infinite and the evolution of human culture and language. Finally, Epicurus considers how we can best understand heavenly phenomena to avoid fear and anxiety and be at peace.*

EPICURUS TO HERODOTUS, GREETING. [35]

I HAVE ALREADY prepared an epitome of my whole system, Herodotus, for those who are unable to study carefully all my writings about nature or to investigate the longer treatises I have composed on the subject. I have done this so they may keep in mind the principal teachings. In this way, whenever the occasion arises, they may be able to aid themselves on the most important points—at least as far as they have taken up the study of nature.

As for those who have made some advance in the survey of the whole system, they should fix in mind an elementary outline of the whole treatment of the subject. After all, in comparison with a comprehensive view of things, the details are rarely necessary.

[36] We must continually return to and memorize this elementary outline for a few reasons. One, doing so will help us to obtain a valid understanding of the facts. Two, once we have rightly understood and mastered the outline, we will have the means by which we may discover all the other details. It is the privilege of the mature student to make a ready use of his apprehensions or perceptions by referring every one of them to elementary facts and simple terms. It is impossible, after all, to gather up the results of an ongoing, diligent study of the entirety of things, unless we can summarize in short formulas and hold in mind all that may be accurately expressed down to the smallest detail.

[37] Therefore, since such a course is of service to all who take up natural science, I, who devote my continuous energy to the subject and reap the calm enjoyment of a life like this, have prepared for you such an epitome and manual of the doctrines as a whole.

GENERAL METHOD—TERMS AND CRITERIA

In the first place, Herodotus, we must understand what each word means. This way we will be in the position to test opinions, inquiries, or problems by utilizing the meaning of each word. Accordingly, our proofs will not run on untested endlessly, nor will the terms we use be empty of meaning. [38] The primary sense of every term employed must be clearly understood. It should require no demonstration. That way we will have a foundation or reference point for the issue, problem, or opinion before us.

Next, we must by all means stick to our sensations, that is, simply to the present impressions—whether of the mind or of any criterion whatsoever—and similarly to our actual feelings. This way we may have the means of determining that which needs confirmation and that which is obscure.

THE EVERLASTING AND UNLIMITED NATURE OF THE COSMOS AND ITS CONSTITUENT PARTS

Now that we have clearly understood these things, it is time to consider some general points that are obscure.

To begin with, nothing comes into being out of what is non-existent. Otherwise, everything could come into being from everything, and there would be no need for any seeds.

[39] Next, if that which disappears is so absolutely destroyed so that it ceases to exist, then everything would soon perish since the disappearing things would be dissolved into that which is non-existent.

Furthermore, the sum total of things—which is to say, everything—was always the same as it is now, and such it will always remain. The reason for this is that there is nothing else into which it can change. For there is nothing beyond the sum total of things that can enter it in order to produce the change.

Moving on, the sum total of things consists of bodies and void.[1] The existence of bodies is everywhere attested by sensation itself. And recall, reason must rely on sensation when it attempts to infer the unknown from the known. [40] And if there were not the void—that which we also call "place" and "intangible nature"—bodies would have nothing in which to be and through which to move, as they are plainly seen to move. Beyond bodies and the void, there is nothing that we can conceive to exist, whether by mental apprehension or by means of analogy.

When we speak of bodies and the void, both are regarded as wholes or separate things, not as the properties or accidents of wholes or separate things. Regarding bodies, some are composite, and others are the elements out of which these composite bodies are made.[2] [41] These elements are indivisible and unchangeable. Otherwise, everything would eventually be destroyed and pass into non-existence. As it is, however, everything is strong enough to endure when the composite bodies are broken up because the elements possess a solid nature and are incapable of being anywhere or in any way dissolved. It follows, therefore, that the first things must be indivisible, corporeal entities.

To make another point, the sum of things is infinite. For that which is finite has an extremity, and the extremity of anything is discernable only in comparison with something else. Since the sum of things has no discernable extremity, it has no limit. And since it has no limit, it must be unlimited or infinite.

Moreover, the sum of things is unlimited both in terms of the multitude of bodies and the magnitude of the void. [42] For if the void were infinite and bodies finite, then the bodies would not have remained in position anywhere. Rather, they would have been scattered in their flight through the infinite void, not having any supports or counterchecks to stabilize them after ricocheting off other bodies. On the other hand, if the void were finite, then the infinite number of bodies would not have anywhere to be.

Furthermore, the indivisible bodies, full as they are since they have no emptiness in them—the atoms out of which composite bodies arise and into which they are dissolved—vary indefinitely in their shapes. For the great variety of things we see could never have come into being out of a recurrence of a definite number of the same shapes. Atoms of each shape, those that are like one another in shape, are absolutely infinite in number. On the other hand, the variety of shapes, though indefinitely large, is not absolutely infinite.[3]

[43] Atoms are in continual motion through the ages.[4] Some of them rebound to a considerable distance from other atoms, while others merely oscillate in one place when they happen to get entangled with or are enclosed by a mass of other atoms shaped for entangling. [44] This oscillation occurs because each atom is separated from the rest by the void, which is incapable of offering any resistance to the rebound. By contrast, it is the solidity of the atom that makes it rebound after a collision, however short the distance to which it rebounds when it finds itself imprisoned in a mass of entangling atoms. There is no beginning of this since both the atoms and the void are forever existent.[5]

[45] The rehearsal at such length of all that we are now recalling to mind furnishes an adequate outline for our conception of the nature of existing things.

But one last related point. There is an infinite number of worlds, some like this world and others unlike it. This is so because the atoms, being infinite in number as has just been demonstrated, are transported ever further in their course. For the atoms out of which a world might arise, or by which a world might be formed, have not all been expended on one world or a finite number of worlds, whether like or unlike this one. So then, there is nothing that prevents an infinity of worlds.

SENSE PERCEPTION—SEEING, HEARING, AND SMELLING

Seeing [46] Moving on, there are impressions—outlines or films of things—that have the same shape as solid bodies, even though they differ from them in their thinness in a way that far exceeds the thinness of any other object we see. For it is not impossible that there should be found in the surrounding air combinations of this kind—materials adapted for expressing the hollowness and thinness of surfaces, and effluxes preserving the same relative position and motion that they had in the solid objects from which they come. We give the name "images" to these outlines or films.

Furthermore, so long as nothing comes in the way to offer resistance, motion through the void accomplishes any imaginable distance in an inconceivably short period of time. This is so because resistance encountered is the same as slowness, whereas the absence of resistance is the same as speed.

[47] By the way, if we consider the minute times perceptible by reason alone, the moving body itself simultaneously arrives at more than one place. But this is impossible. That said, it does arrive simultaneously in time perceptible by sensation, however different the point of departure is from that conceived by us. For if it changed its direction, that would be equivalent to its meeting with resistance, even if up to that point we allow nothing to impede the rate of its flight. This is an elementary fact that, in itself, is well worth keeping in mind.

In the next place, the exceeding thinness of the images is contradicted by none of the facts that we may observe. Consequently, their velocities are also enormous since they find an easy passage everywhere. Moreover, their endless emanation encounters no resistance, or very little—even though many atoms, not to say an unlimited number, do at once encounter resistance.

[48] One should also keep in mind that the production of the images is as quick as thought. For particles are continually flowing from the surface of bodies, even though no reduction of the bodies is observed because other particles take their place. And those given off preserve for a long time the position and arrangement that their atoms had when they formed part of the solid bodies—although occasionally they are thrown into confusion. Sometimes such images are formed very rapidly in the air, as they do not require any solid content. And there are other modes in which they may be formed. Regardless, there is nothing in all this that is contradicted by sensation—if we look at the clear evidence of sensation, to which we should also refer the continuity of particles in the objects that are external to us.

[49] We must also consider that it is by the entrance of something coming from external objects that we see their shapes and think of them. For external objects would not stamp on us their own nature of color and shape—whether through the air, which is between the external things and us, or by means of rays of light, or by currents of any sort going from us to the externals—if certain films or images coming from the things themselves, and thus having the same color and shape as the external things themselves, did not enter into our eyes or minds, into whichever one their size is suitable.

[50] These images move with rapid motion. This explains why they present the appearance of a single continuous object when they strike our senses, and why they retain the original relationship they had with the object. The impact is due to the oscillation of the atoms deep within the solid object from which the images come. And whatever presentation we receive by direct contact—whether it is with the mind or with the sense organs, and whether it is the shape that is presented or other accidents—this presentation is the shape of the solid thing itself and is due either to a close coherence of the image as a whole or to a mere remnant of its parts. Falsehood and error, therefore, are always based on judgment added to a presentation that awaits confirmation or, at least, no contradiction. In the latter case, the presentation remains unconfirmed or even contradicted.[6]

[51] So it is that the mental images we receive (even as mirrors receive images)—whether they arise in our sleep, or whether they are perceived by some other apprehension or perception of the mind or by one of the other criteria of judgement—these mental images would never have resembled what we call real and true things if we had not first come into contact with certain actual things. On the other hand, error would not have occurred if we had not experienced some other movement in ourselves conjoined with, but distinct from, the apprehension or perception of what is presented. Falsehood results from this movement—if it is not confirmed or if it is contradicted. By contrast, if it is confirmed, or if it is not contradicted, then truth is the result.

[52] We must closely adhere to this view so that the criteria of judgment based on clear and distinct perceptions will not be annulled, and so that we will avoid throwing all these things into confusion by maintaining falsehood as if it were the truth.

Hearing The next point. Hearing takes place when a current passes from the object—whether a person or something else—that emits voice or sound or noise, or produces the sensation of hearing in any way whatsoever. This current is broken up into homogeneous particles, which simultaneously preserve a certain mutual connection and a distinctive unity that extends back to the object that emitted them. This current, then, causes the perception of the external object in most cases, or, at the very least, it indicates its presence. [53] And without the transmission of this mutual connection and distinctive unity, no sensation such as this could arise. Therefore, we must not suppose that the air itself is molded into some shape by means of the emitted voice or something similar—for it is hardly the case that the air is acted upon by voice in this way. Instead, the blow that is struck in us when we utter a sound causes such a displacement of particles that it produces a current resembling breath. And this displacement gives rise to the sensation of hearing.

Smelling Moving on, we must believe that smelling, as with hearing, would produce no sensation without particles moving from the object—the right kind of particles that excite the organ utilized in smelling—some bringing confusing and unfamiliar smells, while some carry familiar smells without any confusion.

ATOMS—QUALITIES, PARTS, AND MOTION

[54] Moreover, we must hold that the atoms in fact possess none of the qualities belonging to things that appear to us except shape, weight, and size, and whatever is necessarily associated with shape. For every quality changes, but the atoms do not change since, when the composite bodies are dissolved, there must necessarily be a permanent something, solid and indissoluble, left behind that makes change possible. I do not mean change into or from the non-existent. Rather, I mean that change which happens most often by means of different arrangements and sometimes through the addition or subtraction of atoms. Therefore, these *somethings* that can be diversely arranged must be indestructible, exempt from change, while retaining their own distinctive bulk and shape. These, at the very least, must remain. [55] We see a similar case with what we experience every day. When things fall apart, we can more often than not recognize the shape of the parts that remain of the thing, whereas the thing's qualities vanish. So it is that what is left behind at the dissolution of a body is sufficient to account for the differences in composite bodies. As I said, something must remain and be immune from destruction.

Furthermore, you should not suppose that the atoms have any and every size—or you may be contradicted by phenomena. Rather, we must admit differences of size in order to make it easier to explain our feelings and sensations. [56] But I repeat—it is not necessary to attribute every magnitude to atoms in order to explain qualitative differences. Anyway, if atoms came in all sizes, then we would have by now encountered an atom large enough to see. But we have never observed this—nor can we conceive how an atom could become visible.

Besides, you must not suppose that there are an unlimited number of parts, no matter how small, in any finite body. And so, we must reject as impossible the unlimited cutting and division of a finite body into smaller and smaller parts. For to go down such a path would result in reducing everything to nothing. In that case, we would be forced to admit that the existent things that make up compound bodies—which is to say, atoms—can be reduced to non-existence. Furthermore, no finite body can be transformed again and again *ad infinitum* into smaller and smaller parts. [57] It is impossible to imagine how a finite body would remain limited in size if we posit that an infinite number of particles, however small, are contained in the body. For clearly this infinite number of particles would have some size. And so, whatever size these particles have in themselves, the total amassed body they make would be infinite. Moreover, since what is finite has an extremity, or a limiting edge, that is distinguishable—even if this extremity is not by itself observable—we necessarily think of another such extremity next to or besides the first limiting edge. Considering matters in this way, we can proceed in thought from one limited thing to another until we arrive at infinity.

[58] We must understand that the minimum part or thing perceptible by sense does not correspond to that which can be traversed. Nor is it utterly unlike such a thing. It has something in common with things that can be traversed, though it does not have parts. But when, thanks to the illusion created by this commonality, we think we see another part in the minimum thing—a part on one side and another part on the other side—we must actually be seeing another minimum thing equal to the first. In point of fact, we see minimum things one after another, beginning with the first minimum thing. We do not observe them as occupying the same space nor as touching one another's parts with their own parts. Rather, as unitary indivisibles they provide a means of measuring magnitudes. If the measured magnitude is greater, there are more of them. If smaller, then less.

[59] We must recognize that this analogy also holds for the minimum in the atom. It is only in the atom's scale of size—that is, the atom's very small size—that it differs from that which is observed by sensation. Still, it follows the same analogy. We have declared that atoms have magnitude based upon the analogy of things within our experience. And this magnitude, as small as it is, we

have merely reproduced on a larger scale. Furthermore, the least and simplest things—that is, uncompounded things—must be regarded as extremities of lengths. As a unity, they provide the means for measuring lengths, whether greater lengths or smaller. This sort of measurement is accomplished by means of mental vision since direct observation is impossible. For the similarity that exists between the minimum in the atom and minimum things perceptible to sense is sufficient to justify the conclusion so far as it goes. But it is not possible that the smallest parts of the atom group themselves together through the possession of motion.

[60] Further, we must not assert *up* or *down* of that which is infinite or unlimited as if there were a zenith or nadir, that is, a highest or lowest point. As for the space overhead, however, if it is possible to draw a line to infinity from the point where we stand, we know that this space will never appear to us to be at the same moment up and down with reference to the same point (the point where we stand). The same goes for the space below the hypothetical standpoint and the same kind of infinite line. Judging that it is both up and down at the same moment with reference to the same point is inconceivable. Therefore, it is possible to assume one direction of motion that we conceive as extending upward without limit, and another direction that we conceive as downward, even if our upward motion from our beginning point reaches the feet—or downward motion—of those above us, or our downward motion reaches the heads—or upward motion—of those below us. Nonetheless, the whole of the motion in each case is conceived as extending in opposite directions *ad infinitum*.

[61] Atoms necessarily move with equal speed when travelling through the void without meeting resistance. Heavy atoms will not travel quicker than small and light ones—assuming nothing encounters them. Nor will small atoms travel quicker than large ones if they find a passage suitable to their size, and if they are not obstructed in their movement. Nor will their upward or their lateral motion, which is due to collisions, nor their downward motion, which is due to weight, affect their speed. As long as there is either motion, it must continue at a speed as fast as thought itself as long

as there is no obstruction, whether due to external collision or to the atom's own weight in counteracting the force of the blow.

[62] Furthermore, in composite bodies, one atom will travel faster than another, although their atoms have equal speed. This is because the atoms in the aggregates are travelling in one direction during the shortest continuous time, even though they move in different directions in times so short as to be appreciable only by reason, but frequently collide until the continuity of their motion is appreciated by sensation. For the assumption that beyond the range of direct observation even the minute times conceivable by reason will present continuity of motion is not true in the case before us. Our canon is that direct observation by sense and direct apprehension by the mind are alone invariably true.

THE SOUL—ITS NATURE AND ROLE IN SENSATION

[63] Next, keeping in view our sensations and feelings—since in this way we will have the surest grounds for confidence—we must generally recognize that the soul is a bodily thing composed of fine particles dispersed throughout the whole assemblage of atoms in the human organism.

The soul most nearly resembles wind with an admixture of heat. It is like wind in some ways and heat in others. But there is the third part that exceeds the other two in the fineness of its particles and thereby keeps in closer touch with the rest of the human organism. This is shown by the powers of the soul, its feelings, the ease with which it moves, its thought processes, and by all those things we lose when we die.

We must keep in mind that the soul has the greatest share in causing sensation. [64] Nevertheless, if it had not been somehow confined within the rest of the human organism, it would not have had sensation. Still, the rest of the human organism has its own soul-derived share of the ability—even though it provides the indispensable condition for the soul. And yet it does not possess all the properties of the soul. And so, on the departure of the soul it loses sensation. This is so because it does not have this power in itself. Rather, something else that came into being with it supplied it to the body. This other thing—through the power actualized in it by means of motion—at once acquired for itself the property of sense perception. And because of its proximity to and affinity with the body, this other thing imparted it, as I said, to the body.

[65] Hence, as long as the soul is in the body, it never loses sensation through the removal of some other part. The container may be dislocated in whole or in part, and portions of the soul may thereby be lost. Despite this, the soul will nevertheless retain sensation if it manages to survive. But as soon as those atoms that make up the nature of the soul have departed—however few—the rest of the human organism no longer has sensation, whether the whole of it survives or only a part. Moreover, when the whole of the human organism is broken up, the soul is scattered and no longer has the same powers as before, nor the same motions. Therefore, the soul no longer possesses sensation.

[66] This is so because we cannot think of the soul as sensing without it being in this composite whole and moving with these movements. Nor can we think of it in this manner whenever the containers that enclose and surround it are not the same as those in which the soul is now located and in which it performs these movements.[7]

[67] There is another point we must consider—the nature of that which is without a body, which is to say incorporeal. According to the way people now use the term *incorporeal*, it can be thought of as self-existent. But aside from the void, it is impossible to think of anything incorporeal as self-existent. And the void itself is able neither to act nor be acted on, but it simply allows bodies to move through it. Therefore, those who call the soul incorporeal speak foolishly. For if the soul were incorporeal, it would be able neither to act nor be acted on. As it is, however, both these properties manifestly belong to the soul.

[68] If, then, we bring all these arguments concerning the soul to the criteria of our feelings and sensations, and if we keep in mind the proposition stated at the beginning, we will see that the subject has been adequately set out in outline. This will enable us to determine

the details with accuracy and confidence.

PROPERTIES AND ACCIDENTS[8] — INCLUDING TIME

Moving on, the shapes, colors, magnitudes, and weights — in short, all those things that are predicated of body as accidents either of all things or of visible things — are knowable by sensation itself. We must not think of these as existing independently in themselves — for that is inconceivable — [69] nor as being non-existent, nor as being some other and incorporeal entity inhering in the body, nor again as being parts of it. We must hold that the whole body in a general way derives its permanent nature from all these — though the body is not, as it were, formed by grouping these together in the same way that a larger aggregate is made up from the particles themselves, whether these particles be primary or any magnitudes whatsoever less than the whole aggregate. All these, I repeat, merely give the body its own permanent nature. They all have their own characteristic modes of being perceived and distinguished — but always along with the whole body in which they inhere, and never apart from it. It is on account of this complete conception of the body as a whole that it is designated *body*.

[70] Properties often attach to bodies without being permanent aspects. These are neither invisible nor incorporeal. Therefore, using the term as it is commonly used, we make it clear that these properties do not have the nature of the whole thing to which they belong (that which, conceiving it as a whole, we give the name of body), nor do they have the nature of the permanent aspects without which we cannot think of a body. And because of certain peculiar modes of apprehension into which the complete body always enters, each of them can be called by this name — [71] but only as often as they are seen actually to belong to it, since such properties are not permanent aspects. There is no need to banish from reality the clear evidence that these properties do not have the nature of that whole — by us called body — to which it belongs, nor of the permanent aspects that accompany the whole. Nor, on the other hand, must we suppose that they have independent existence (for this is

just as inconceivable in their case as in the case of the permanent accidents). But—as is manifest—they should all be regarded as properties of bodies rather than as permanent aspects that accompany bodies. Nor do they independently exist. Rather they are seen to be exactly as and what sensation itself makes them individually claim to be.

[72] There is another point we must consider carefully. We must not investigate time as we do the other things that we investigate in an object, namely, by referring them to the preconceptions envisaged in our minds. Rather, we must take into account the clearly perceived phenomenon by which we speak of time as long or short, linking it closely to our experience. We do not need to adopt any novel terms as preferable, but we should employ the usual expressions in reference to time. Nor do we need to predicate anything else of time as if this something else contained the same essence as is contained in the proper meaning of the word time. This, after all, is done by some. We must chiefly consider what we associate with time and that by which we measure time. [73] The matter requires no further demonstration. We need only to reflect on the fact that we associate time with days and nights and their parts, and similarly to feelings and the lack of feelings, and to states of movement and states of rest. And so, we understand that a distinct property of these is what we call time.[9]

THE RISE OF OTHER WORLDS AND THE EVOLUTION OF HUMAN LANGUAGES

In addition to the foregoing points I have made, we should consider that the worlds and every other finite aggregate that bears a strong resemblance to things we commonly see have come into being out of the infinite. All these, whether great or small, have been separated off from distinct gatherings of atoms. And all things will be dissolved again—some faster, some slower, some through the action of one set of causes, others through the action of another set.[10] [74] Moreover, we must not suppose that the worlds necessarily have one and the same shape.[11] For no one can demonstrate that in one sort of world there might not be contained the seeds out of which animals and plants arise, as well as everything else we see, whereas in another sort of world there could not possibly be these seeds.[12]

[75] Again, we must suppose that human nature was compelled by circumstances to learn many things of different kinds. And reason subsequently developed what it had received and made additional discoveries. The developments moved along at a quicker pace among some peoples and at a slower pace among others. So it was that the progress made at times was great, and at other times less so.

Therefore, even the names of, or words for, things did not originally spring into being thanks to convention. Instead, each unique ethnic group of human beings produced them when they were affected by distinct feelings and received distinct apparitions. The air emitted in this way was shaped by these distinct feelings and apparitions, and in different ways depending on the variety of lands inhabited by the different groups of people. [76] Subsequently, whole ethnic groups adopted their own special terms so that their communications might be less ambiguous to one another and more briefly expressed. As for things not generally known, or things unseen, those who were aware of them tried to introduce these things by circulating certain terms for them. These names were either instinctively uttered sounds spoken under a kind of compulsion, or they were selected in a more rational fashion, based on analogy and according to general usage.

HOW TO UNDERSTAND HEAVENLY PHENOMENA SO AS TO AVOID FEAR AND ANXIETY AND BE AT PEACE

Moving on, as for things in the sky, we should acknowledge that revolutions and solstices and eclipses and risings and settings and the like take place without the administration or command, either now or in the future, of some being that simultaneously enjoys perfect bliss as well as indestructibility. [77] This is so because practical troubles and anxieties and feelings of anger and the granting of favors do

not accord with bliss, but always imply weakness and fear and de-
pendence upon one's neighbors. Nor should we hold that these
things in the sky, which are no more than globular masses of fire,
enjoy bliss or that they assume these motions at will. No, in every
term we use, we must hold fast to all the majesty that attaches to such
notions. Otherwise, the terms will generate opinions inconsistent
with this majesty, and such inconsistency will be enough to produce
the most disturbing confusion in our souls. Therefore, where we find
regularly recurring phenomena, we must assign the regularity of the
recurrence to the original interception and conglomeration of atoms
by which the cosmos was formed.

[78] Furthermore, we must hold that the function of the study
of natural phenomena is to clearly understand the cause of the most
important things. And we must hold that blessed happiness depends on this, and on knowing what the heavenly bodies really are,
and any similar knowledge that would contribute to a clear understanding. Moreover, relative to such points as these, we must recognize that there is no plurality of causes or contingency. Rather,
we must hold that nothing suggestive of conflict or disturbing confusion is compatible with an indestructible and blessed nature. The
mind can grasp the simple truth of this.

[79] But when we come to subjects for special inquiry, there is
nothing in the knowledge of risings and settings and solstices and
eclipses and every similar subject that contributes to our blessed
happiness. On the contrary, those who know about such matters,
while remaining ignorant about the true nature of the heavenly
phenomena or the most important causes, feel just as much fear as
those who do not have special knowledge. Actually, it is possible to
say that they feel an even greater fear when the feeling of astonish-
ment stirred up by this additional knowledge cannot find a solution
or understand how these phenomena depend on the highest causes.

Therefore, if we discover more than one cause that may possibly
account for solstices, settings and risings, eclipses, and the like,
even as we also found in particular matters of detail, [80] we must
not suppose that our treatment of these matters fails in terms of accuracy—as far as accuracy is required to ensure our tranquility and

blessed happiness, anyway. When, therefore, we investigate the causes of celestial and atmospheric phenomena—as with all that is unknown—we must take into account the variety of ways in which analogous occurrences happen within our experience. We must disregard those who, overlooking the fact that these objects are only seen at a distance, do not recognize the difference between that which is or comes about from a single cause and that which may be the effect of any one of several causes. We must also disregard those who are ignorant of what makes tranquility possible or what prevents it. If, then, we suppose that an event could happen in one particular way or another out of many, then we will be just as tranquil as if we knew with certainty that it happened in one particular way.

[81] There is yet one more point to grasp—namely, that the greatest disturbance arises in the human soul thanks to the belief that the heavenly bodies are blessed and indestructible, while these same bodies simultaneously wish and act and cause in ways that are incompatible with these attributes. Disturbances also arise thanks to the anticipation or suspicion of some everlasting evil—either because of the myths or because we are in dread of the mere insensibility of death, as if it had to do with us. People are reduced to this state not because of conviction but because of a certain irrational tendency. Accordingly, if men do not set limitations on their terror, they must suffer as much or an even more intense anxiety than the man whose views on these matters are quite vague. [82] But mental tranquility means being released from all these troubles and keeping in mind the general and most important points.

Therefore, we must attend to present feelings and sensations, whether those of mankind in general or those peculiar to the individual. We must also attend to all the clear evidence available to us as given by each of the criteria. By paying attention to these, we will correctly and fully be able to explain the source of the disturbance and the fear, banishing it by accounting for celestial phenomena and for all other things that happen to us from time to time—things that cause the utmost fear in the rest of mankind.

· · ·

CONCLUSION

Here then, Herodotus, are the most important points on the whole of nature in summary form. [83] Accordingly, if this statement is accurately retained and the points herein take effect, then I believe that a man will be far better equipped than others—even if he never goes into all the exact details. This is so because he will clear up for himself many of the points that I have worked out in detail in my longer and more complete treatise. The summary will help if one keeps it in mind. It is such that those who are already more or less, or even perfectly, acquainted with the details can, by breaking down what they know into such elementary perceptions as these, successfully pursue their research into the whole of nature. At the same time, those who are not as advanced can silently fashion and as quick as thought run through the teachings most important for the calming of the mind.

DIOGENES LAERTIUS: Such is Epicurus' letter on natural things. Next is his letter on things in the sky.

NOTES

[1] At some point a scholiast, or commentator, added the following (from now on such commentary will simply be noted as "Added commentary:"): "He says this also in the *Larger Epitome* near the beginning and in the first book of *On Nature.*"

[2] Added commentary: "He repeats this in the first book of *On Nature* and in books 14 and 15 of the *Larger Epitome.*"

[3] Added commentary: "For neither does the divisibility go on without end, he says below. And, he adds, since the qualities change, unless one is prepared to keep enlarging their magnitudes also simply without end.'"

[4] Added commentary: "He further says below that the atoms move with equal speed since the void makes way for the lightest and heaviest alike."

[5] Added commentary: "He says below that atoms have no quality at all except shape, size, and weight. He states that color varies with the arrangement of the atoms in his *Twelve Rudiments*. He further says that atoms are not of any and every size. Anyway, no atom has ever been seen by our sense perception."

[6] Added commentary: "Following a certain movement in ourselves connected

with, but distinct from, the mental picture presented—which is the cause of error."

[7] Added commentary: "He says elsewhere that the soul is composed of the smoothest and roundest of atoms, far superior in both respects to those of fire. He says that part of the soul is irrational, this part being scattered over the rest of the frame, while the rational part resides in the chest, as is manifest from our fears and our joy. He says that sleep occurs when the parts of the soul that have been scattered all over the composite organism are held fast in it or dispersed, and afterwards collide with one another by their impacts. The semen is derived from the whole of the body."

[8] Though others (R.D Hicks, Eugene O'Connor, George Strodach) over the past century have translated *sumptōma* and *sumbebēkos* alternatively, and sometimes oppositely, to what we give here, and despite the apparent confusion of *Liddell & Scott's Greek-English Lexicon*, we at the Cave have followed the recent and consistent scholarship of Lloyd P. Gerson (and sometimes Brad Inwood with others) in giving *sumptōma* as "property" and *sumbebēkos* as "accident." That said, the translation does not always seem to work, though the general sense is usually clear.

[9] Added commentary: "He says this both in the second book of *On Nature* and in the *Larger Epitome*."

[10] Added commentary: "It is clear, then, that he also makes the worlds perishable, as their parts are subject to change. Elsewhere he says the earth is supported on the air."

[11] Added commentary: "On the contrary, in the twelfth book of *On Nature*, he himself says that the shapes of the worlds differ, some being spherical, some oval, others again of shapes different from these. They do not, however, admit of every shape. Nor are they living beings that have been separated from the infinite."

[12] Added commentary: "And the same holds good for their nurture in a world after they have arisen. And so too we must think it happens upon the earth also."

ON THINGS IN THE SKY
THE LETTER TO PYTHOCLES

IN BRIEF: *After agreeing to satisfy Pythocles' request for an epitome on phenomena in the sky, and after stating a few methodological principles (we cannot attain the impossible; we cannot understand all matters equally well; "we must not accept empty assumptions and arbitrary laws"; "we should follow the promptings of the phenomena"), along with the reason why such study is important ("tranquility of mind and resolute conviction and confidence"), Epicurus explores the development of the many worlds from the infinite. He goes on to offer various explanations for those things in the sky having to do with the sun, the moon, and other stars: the relative size of the sun and other stars; their rising and setting; why the sun and moon follow particular paths; the waxing and waning of the moon, how it shines, and why a face appears in the moon; eclipses of the sun and moon; why days and nights vary in length. He later discusses comets, and why some stars appear to move, while others appear to remain still or fall. Otherwise, he explores how different earthly, atmospheric, and weather phenomena occur—clouds, rain, thunder, lightning, whirlwinds, earthquakes, winds, hail, snow, dew, frost, ice, rainbows, and lunar halos. Epicurus' point is two-fold. One, there are many possible explanations for these phenomena. Two, one should not resort to mythological accounts to explain them. Since they are perfectly happy, the gods do not concern themselves with such things.*

EPICURUS TO PYTHOCLES, GREETING. [84]

IN YOUR LETTER that Cleon brought to me, you continue to show me an affection that matches my own devotion to you. Moreover, you try—and not without success—to recall the considerations that make for a blessedly happy life.

PYTHOCLES' REQUEST

You ask me for a clear and concise statement about things in the sky—about celestial phenomena—for the sake of aiding your memory. You tell me that the other essays I've written on this subject are hard to remember, though you always have my books with you.

I was delighted to receive your request and am full of pleasant expectations. [85] Consequently, I will complete my writing and grant all you ask.

Many others besides you will find these arguments and explanations useful—especially those who have only recently become acquainted with the true story of the nature of things, as well as those who are deeply preoccupied with the ordinary affairs of life. So, Pythocles, you will do well to take them up and thoroughly learn them along with the short epitome I wrote to Herodotus.

THE METHOD AND THE GOAL

In the first place, remember that, like everything else, knowledge of celestial phenomena—whether taken along with other things or in isolation—has no other purpose than tranquility of mind and resolute conviction and confidence.

[86] We do not seek to wrest by force what is impossible. Nor do we hope to understand all matters equally well. Nor can we make our treatment always as clear as when we discuss human life or explain the other questions regarding nature—for example, that the whole of being consists of bodies and intangible nature, or that the ultimate elements of things are indivisible, or any other proposition that admits only one explanation of the phenomena to be possible.

But this is not the case with things in the sky. As for their occurrence, celestial phenomena allow for more than one cause and a variety of accounts of their existence—none that contradict sensation. [87] In the study of nature, we must not accept empty assumptions and arbitrary laws. Rather, we should follow the promptings of the phenomena, the facts themselves. We have come to the point where our life has no need for non-rational and empty opinion. Our one need is to live undisturbed, without trouble.

As soon as we suitably understand what may be plausibly said of everything—if everything is explained by the method of plurality of causes in conformity with the facts—we will realize that all things go on in an unshakeable manner, consistent and reliable. But when we pick and choose among the causes, rejecting one that is equally consistent with the phenomena, we clearly fall away from the study of nature and tumble into myth.

Some phenomena within our own experience offer evidence by which we may interpret what goes on in the sky. We can observe and contemplate how the former really work but not how the latter celestial phenomena take place since their occurrence may possibly be due to a variety of causes. [88] Regardless, we must observe each thing as it is presented. We must furthermore separate it from all the other things presented along with it, the occurrence of which from various causes is not contradicted by facts within our experience.

THE WORLDS—THEIR NATURE AND DEVELOPMENT

A cosmos or a world is a circumscribed portion of the sky, which contains stars, an earth, and all other visible things. It is cut off from the infinite, terminating in an exterior that may either revolve or be at rest.[1] The world may be round or triangular or of any shape. All these alternatives are possible since they are contradicted by none of the observable facts in this world, in which an extremity can nowhere be discerned.

[89] We may understand that there is an infinite number of such worlds. And more, we may understand that such a world may arise within another world, or in one of the interworlds, a term by which we mean the interval between worlds. This is a place that is relatively empty and not, as some maintain, a vast place that is perfectly clear and void.

A cosmos or a world arises when certain suitable seeds flow in from a single world or interworld, or from several worlds or interworlds for that matter, and undergo gradual additions or articulations or changes of place—as it may be. The worlds receive ongoing inflows from appropriate sources until they are matured and firmly settled insofar as the prepared foundations can receive them. [90] I say this about the inflow because it is not enough—as some believe—that there is an aggregation of atoms, or a vortex in the empty space that comes about by necessity in which a world may arise and grow until it collides with another world—as one of the so-called physicists says. For this conflicts with the facts.

PHENOMENA IN THE SKY—
THE SUN, MOON, PLANETS, AND OTHER STARS

The sun and the moon and the remaining stars did not come into being independently from our world only later to be included in our world.[2] Instead—like the earth and sea—they at once began to take form and grow by the accretions and whirling motions of certain substances of the finest texture, substances having either the nature of wind or fire, or of both. This, anyway, is what sensation suggests.

[91] The size of the sun and the remaining stars relative to us is just as great as it appears.[3] That said, it may be a little larger, or a little smaller, or precisely as great as it is seen to be. So too do fires, which we know from experience, appear when observed by sensation. And every objection brought against this part of the theory will easily be resolved by anyone who attends to the clearly perceived facts—just as I show in my book *On Nature*.

[92] The rising and setting of the sun, moon, and the remaining stars may be due to kindling and quenching, provided that the circumstances are such as to produce these results in each of the two places, east and west. No fact testifies against this. Or the result might be produced by their coming forward above the earth and again by the earth's intervention to hide them. No fact testifies against this either. And their motion may be due to the rotation of the whole sky. Or the sky may be at rest and they alone may rotate according to some necessary impulse to rise implanted when the world was first coming into being . . .[4] [93] and this through excessive heat, due to a certain extension of the fire that always encroaches upon that which is near it.

The turnings of the sun and moon in their course may be due to the obliquity of the sky by which it is forced back at these times. On the other hand, the turnings may equally be due to the contrary pressure of the air or—it is possible, anyway—to the fact that either the fuel necessary from time to time has been consumed in the vicinity or there is a shortage of it. Or it may even be because such a whirling motion was inherent in these stars from the beginning so that they move in a sort of spiral. All such explanations, and similar ones, do not conflict with any clear evidence—as long as we hold fast to what is possible in the details and can bring each of these explanations into an agreement with the facts, unalarmed by the servile artifices of the astronomers.

[94] The waning of the moon, and the waxing that follows, might be due to the rotation of the moon's body—and equally well to formations that the air takes on. Or, again, it may be due to the interposition of certain bodies. In short, it may happen in any of the ways that the facts within our experience suggest it may happen.

One must not be so much in love with explaining things in a single way so as to reject all other ways from ignorance of what is, and what is not, within the reach of human knowledge, and from a consequent longing to discover what is impossible to discover.

Furthermore, the moon may possibly shine by its own light. It is just as possible that it may get its light from the sun. [95] I say this because in our own experience we see many things that shine by their own light and many as well that shine by borrowed light. And none of the celestial phenomena stand in the way.

The latter point is true as long as we always keep in mind the method of plural explanation and the several consistent assumptions and causes, instead of dwelling on what is inconsistent and giving these inconsistencies a false significance so that we always fall back, in one way or another, upon the single explanation.

The appearance of a face in the moon may equally arise from the interchange of various parts, or from the interposition of something, or in any other way that may be understood to agree with the facts.

[96] This method of research should not be abandoned no matter

what it is you are studying in the sky. I say this because if you dispute clearly perceived evidence, you will never be able to have genuine tranquility of mind.

An eclipse of the sun or the moon may be due to the extinction of their light, even as we observe this happening in our own experience. Or the eclipse may happen by the interposition of something else, whether it be the earth or some other invisible body like it. And so, in this way we must consider the explanations that agree with one another and remember that the concurrence of more than one at the same time may possibly happen.[5]

[97] Furthermore, let the regularity of their orbits be explained in the same way as certain ordinary incidents within our own experience. Whatever the case, the divine nature must not be given to explain this. Rather, the divine nature must be kept free from the task and in perfect bliss. Otherwise, the whole study of things in the sky will be pointless. This pointless study has proved to be the case with some who did not utilize the method of possible explanations but fell into the folly of supposing that these events happen in one single way alone, and of rejecting all other ways that are possible. They allowed themselves to be carried into the realm of the unintelligible, unable as they were to take a comprehensive view of the facts—a view that must be taken as clues to the rest.

[98] The variations in the length of nights and days may be due to the swiftness, or yet again to the slowness, of the sun's motion in the sky—which is itself due to the variations in the length of spaces crossed, and to the sun accomplishing some distances more swiftly or more slowly, even as it happens sometimes in our own experience. Our explanation of celestial phenomena must agree with these facts, whereas those who adopt only one explanation are in conflict with the facts and are utterly mistaken regarding how a man can get knowledge.

WEATHER AND OTHER EARTH AND ATMOSPHERIC PHENOMENA

The happenings in the sky that signify the weather may be due to the mere coincidence of the seasons, as is the case with signs from animals seen on earth, or they may be caused by changes and alterations in the air. Neither the one explanation nor the other conflicts with the facts, [99] and it is not easy to see in which cases the effect is due to one cause or to the other.

Clouds may form and gather for several reasons. They may do so because the air is condensed under the pressure of winds. Or because atoms that hold together and are suitable to produce this result become mutually entangled. Or because currents collect from the earth and its waters. It is not impossible that there are several other ways in which clouds may form.

Rain may be produced out of the clouds by means of their compression or by means of their transformation. [100] Then again, rain may be caused by the exhalations of moisture rising from suitable places through the air, while a more violent inundation is due to certain accumulations suitable for such a discharge.

Thunder may be due to the rolling of wind in the hollow parts of the clouds, even as wind is sometimes imprisoned in jars that we use. Or it may be due to the roaring of fire in the clouds when blown by a wind. Or to the rending and disruption of clouds. Or to the friction and splitting up of clouds when they have become as firm as ice.

[101] As in the whole survey, so in this particular point, the facts invite us to give a plurality of explanations.

Lightning similarly may arise in a variety of ways. For when the clouds rub against one another and collide, the collocation of atoms that is the cause of fire generates lightning. Or it may be due to particles capable of producing this brightness flashing out from the clouds due to the winds. Or lightning is squeezed out of the clouds when they have been condensed either by their own action or by that of the winds. Or, yet again, the light diffused from the stars may be enveloped in the clouds, then driven about by their motion and by that of the winds, before finally making its escape from the clouds. Or light of the finest texture may be filtered through the clouds (whereby the clouds may be set on fire and thunder produced), and the motion of this light may make lightning. Or it may arise from the combustion of wind brought about by the violence of its motion and the intensity of its compression. [102] Or, when the clouds are torn apart by winds, and the atoms which generate fire are expelled, these likewise cause lightning to appear. And so, it may easily be observed that the occurrence of lightning is possible in many other ways, just as long as we always hold on to the facts and take a general view of what is analogous to them.

When the clouds are arranged as I mentioned above, lightning precedes thunder because the configuration that produces lightning is expelled at the moment when the wind falls upon the cloud. And the roar of thunder is produced by the wind being rolled up afterwards. Or, if both are simultaneous, the lightning moves with a greater velocity towards us, [103] and the thunder lags behind, exactly as when persons who are striking blows are observed from a distance.

A thunderbolt is caused when winds are repeatedly collected, imprisoned, and violently ignited. Or when a part is torn off and more violently expelled downwards—the tearing due to the fact that the compression of the clouds has made the neighboring parts denser. Or, again, as with thunder, it may be due merely to the expulsion of the imprisoned fire, when this has accumulated and been more violently inflated with wind and has torn the cloud, being unable to withdraw to the adjacent parts since it is continually more and more closely compressed.[6]

[104] There are in addition several other ways in which thunderbolts may possibly be produced. The exclusion of myth is the sole condition necessary. And myth will be excluded if one properly attends to the facts in order to draw inferences about what is obscure.

Whirlwinds are due to the descent of a cloud forced downward like a pillar by the wind in full force and carried by a gale around and around, while at the same time the outside wind gives the cloud a lateral thrust. Or whirlwinds may be due to a change of the wind that forms into a circle as a current of air from above forces it to move. Or it may be that a strong whirling of winds has begun and is unable to burst through to the side because the air surrounding it is closely condensed. [105] When whirlwinds fall upon land, they cause what are called turn-abouts, or tornadoes, in agreement with the various ways in which they are produced through the force of the wind. And when whirlwinds fall upon the sea, they cause waterspouts.

Earthquakes may be due to the imprisonment of wind underground, and to its being interspersed with small masses of earth and then set in continuous motion, therefore causing the earth to tremble. The earth either takes in this wind from the outside, or when the earth's foundations are undermined and fall into subterranean caverns, a wind is stirred up in the imprisoned air. Or earthquakes may be due to the spread of movement arising from the fall of many such earth foundations and to these masses of earth being again checked when they encounter the more solid resistance of earth. [106] And there are many other causes that may explain these oscillations of the earth.

Winds arise from time to time when foreign matter continually and gradually finds its way into the air, and through the gathering of great amounts of water. The rest of the winds arise when a few of them fall into the many hollows and are in this way divided and multiplied.

Hail is caused by the stronger condensation of certain particles resembling wind—the result of their complete transformation and subsequent distribution into drops—and also by the slighter solidification of certain particles of moisture and their simultaneous cracking, which simultaneously forces them together and makes them burst, so that they become frozen in parts and in the whole mass. [107] It is possible that the round shape of hailstones is due to the melting of their extremities on all sides, and to the fact that, when the hailstones are formed, particles of moisture or wind evenly surround them on all sides.

Snow may be formed when a fine rain pours out from the clouds through symmetrical passageways when winds violently pressurize suitable clouds. Then this rain is frozen on the way because of some violent change in coldness in the region below the clouds. Yet again, by means of condensation in clouds that have uniform density, a fall of snow might occur through the clouds that contain densely packed moisture in close proximity to one another. And these clouds produce a sort of compression and cause hail, which happens mostly in spring. [108] And when frozen clouds rub against one another, this accumulation of snow might be thrown off. And there are other ways in which snow might be formed.

Dew is formed when such particles as are capable of producing this sort of moisture meet one another from the air. Or it is formed by these particles rising from moist and damp places—the sort of place where dew is chiefly formed—and their subsequent combination, so as to create moisture and fall downwards. We observe something similar take place before our eyes in several cases.

[109] The formation of frost is no different from that of dew—certain particles of such a nature become in some such way condensed due to a certain condition of cold air.

Ice is formed by the expulsion of circular shaped particles from the water, while the scalene and acute-angled shaped atoms contained in it are compressed. It is further formed by the buildup of such atoms from the outside. These compressed atoms cause the water to solidify after the expulsion of a certain number of round atoms.

The rainbow develops when the sun shines upon humid air. Or it may arise by some unusual blending of light with air, which causes either all the distinctive qualities of these colors or some of them belonging to a single kind. Or it may be that from the reflection of this light, the air all around is colored as we see it when the sun shines upon its parts. [110] The circular shape of the rainbow is due to the fact that the distance of every point is perceived by our sight to be equal. Or the circular shape may be due to the combination of the atoms that presents a sort of roundness—the atoms in the air, or in the clouds, and those originating with the sun, having thus been united in this way.

A halo arises around the moon when the air is carried from all sides to the moon. Or it does because it evenly carries the air currents up from the moon so high that it impresses a circle upon the cloudy mass without separating it altogether. Or because it raises the air that immediately surrounds the moon symmetrically from all sides up to a circumference around the moon, and there it forms a thick ring. [111] This happens in certain portions either because a current has forced its way in from the outside or because the heat has gained possession of certain passages in order to produce this effect.

OTHER SKY PHENOMENA

Stars with long hair, or comets, arise when, if circumstances are favorable, fire is nourished in certain places at certain intervals of time in the sky. Or because at times the sky has a particular motion above us so that such stars appear. Or because the stars themselves at times are set in motion under certain conditions and come to our region in the sky and make their appearance. Their disappearance is due to the causes that are the opposite of these.

[112] Some stars revolve without setting not only for the reason alleged by some—because this is the part of the world around which, itself unmoved, the rest revolves—but it may also be because a circular revolution of air surrounds this part, which prevents them from travelling out of sight like other stars. Or it is possible that there is a shortage of necessary matter for fuel in other areas, while there is an abundance in that area where they are seen. There are in addition several other ways by which this might happen, as may be seen by anyone capable of reasoning in accordance with the facts.

The wandering of certain stars, if such wandering is their actual motion, and the regular movement of certain other stars, [113] may be accounted for by saying that they originally moved in a circle and were constrained—some of them to be turned around with the same uniform rotation and others with a turning motion that varied. Yet it may also be that—given the diversity of the regions crossed—in some places there are uniform tracts of air that force the stars forward in one direction, the stars burning uniformly, while in other places these tracts are so irregular that they cause the observed motions. To assign a single cause for these effects, when the facts suggest several causes, is madness and an improper practice—yet it is done by adherents of a certain groundless kind of astronomy, who offer empty explanations for the stars whenever they refuse to liberate the divine nature from troublesome duties.

[114] That some stars appear to be left behind by others may be due to the fact that, even though they go around the same circle as the others, they travel more slowly. Or it may be that they are drawn back by the same whirling motion and move in the opposite direction. Or, yet again, it may be that some travel over a larger region, and others over one that is smaller, in travelling around the same circle. But to declare as certain a single explanation of these phenomena is worthy of those who seek to dazzle the multitude with marvels.

Falling stars, as they are called, may in some cases be due to the mutual friction of the stars themselves. They may occur in other cases because of the expulsion of certain parts upon the mixture of fire and air that was mentioned when we were discussing lightning. [115] Or it may be because of the meeting of atoms capable of generating fire, atoms that accord so well that they produce this result as well as the subsequent motion, wherever the impulse that first brought them together leads them. Or it may be that wind collects in certain dense mist-like masses, and, since it is imprisoned, the wind ignites and then bursts out upon whatever is nearby it, being carried to that place where the impulse carries it. And there are other ways these things can happen—none of them having anything to do with myth.

DOUBTFUL WEATHER SIGNS

The fact that the weather is sometimes foretold utilizing the behavior of certain animals is a mere coincidence in time. For the animals offer no necessary reason why a storm should be produced. And no divine being sits observing when these animals go out and afterward fulfilling the signs that the animals have given. [116] Such folly would not even occur to the most ordinary, slightly graced being, much less one who enjoys perfect happiness.

CONCLUSION

You should keep all this in mind, Pythocles, in order to move far away from myth, and so that you will be able to understand cases similar to these.

Above all, give yourself over to the study of first things and of infinity and of similar matters, as well as to the exploration of the criteria by which we judge, and of the feelings, and of the goal for which we make our considerations. For if you study these things together, you will easily be able to understand the causes of the particular phenomena. Those who have not fully accepted these points, in proportion as they have not done so, will not be able to study these matters very well, nor will they be able to achieve the goal for which they should be studied.

[117] DIOGENES LAERTIUS: Such are Epicurus' views on things in the sky.

NOTES

[1] Added commentary: "And terminating in a boundary that may be either thick or thin, a boundary whose dissolution will bring about the ruin of all within it."

[2] Added commentary: "Such parts of it, at least, as serve at all for its preservation."

[3] Added commentary: "This he states in the eleventh book of *On Nature*. For if, he says, it had diminished in size because of the distance, it would have diminished its brightness much more. For indeed there is no distance more proportionate to this diminution of size than is the distance at which the brightness begins to diminish."

[4] There is likely a missing portion, a lacuna, here in the text.

[5] Added commentary: "He says the same in Book 12 of his *On Nature*, and further that the sun is eclipsed when the moon throws her shadow over him, and the moon is eclipsed by the shadow of the earth. But an eclipse also may be due to the moon's withdrawal. And this is also cited by Diogenes the Epicurean in the first book of his *Selections*."

[6] Added commentary: "Generally by some high mountain where thunderbolts mostly fall."

PART 2

ETHICS
HOW TO LIVE WELL & BE HAPPY

ON LIVING WELL & HAPPILY
THE LETTER TO MENOECEUS

IN BRIEF: *Epicurus suggests that everyone should study philosophy in order to be happy. One should practice living well by keeping a few key truths in mind and making choices in keeping with these. The first truth is that the gods are blessed and indestructible and nothing to the contrary. The second is that death means nothing to human beings. The wise person seeks merely to enjoy life. And yet—the third truth—we should not seek to satisfy every desire since only the satisfaction of some is necessary for happiness. The goal is bodily health and mental tranquility. Thus, we seek freedom from pain and fear. For this reason, Epicurus discusses the fourth truth, that of pleasure and pain. Not every pleasure is chosen and not every pain is rejected. The best life is the simple life centered on natural and necessary desires and trouble-free pleasures. Practical wisdom and the other virtues aid one in living this life.*

DIOGENES LAERTIUS: [117] As for those things having to do with human life, what we should choose and what we should avoid, Epicurus writes as follows: . . .[1] [121]

EPICURUS TO MENOECEUS, GREETING. [122]

L ET NO ONE put off studying philosophy when he is young, nor become weary of it when he is old, for no age is too early or too late for the health of the soul. To suggest that the time for studying philosophy has not yet come or that it is long gone is like saying that it is too early or too late for happiness. Therefore, both the young and the old should seek wisdom. The latter should do philosophy so that, even though he is old, he may be young in good things through the delight of what has been, whereas the former should do philosophy so that, while he is still young, he may at the same time be old through his lack of fear of what is destined to come. So, we must practice those things that produce happiness since if happiness is present, we possess everything, and if it is not, we do everything to acquire it.

THE BASIC ELEMENTS OF LIVING WELL

[123] Do and practice those things that I have continually recommended to you, taking them to be the basic elements of living well.

The Gods

First, you should acknowledge that the god is an indestructible and blessed living being. This is the commonly held understanding of the god, the common epithet in writing. Accordingly, do not attribute to him anything that is contrary to his indestructibility or incongruous with his blessed happiness. Instead, think about the god whatever can defend and uphold his blessed happiness and his indestructibility.[2]

I say this because there are gods. And knowledge related to them is manifest. But the gods are not such as the many customarily believe since the many do not carefully guard and thus maintain a consistent view about the gods. The impious man is not the one who denies the gods of the many; rather, the impious man is the one who adheres to the opinions of the many about the gods. [124] This is so because the assertions of the many about the gods are not true preconceptions but false assumptions.

So it is that the greatest harms come to bad men from the gods, while the greatest benefits come to good men. For the gods always receive those men who are like them since they make every virtue their own, while rejecting everything that does not belong to them.

Death

You should get used to the idea that death means nothing to us.

This is so because every good and every evil is connected to sensation. And death is the loss of all sensation.

It follows that a right understanding of the fact that death means nothing to us makes the mortal nature of life beneficial to us—not by adding to life an unlimited amount of time, but by taking away the yearning for immortality. [125] For there is no terror at all in living for the one who has thoroughly grasped that there is no terror at all in not living. Foolish, therefore, is the man who says that he fears death because it pains him to think about its eventual coming rather than actually paining him when it comes. Whatever causes no trouble when it is present causes only a groundless pain in its mere anticipation.

So then, death—that evil which most causes us to shudder— means nothing to us since when we exist, death is not present, and when death is present, we do not exist. In fact, death means nothing either to the living or to those who have finished living since it does not exist for the former, and the latter no longer exist. Nevertheless, most people flee death as the greatest of evils. Yet at other times they choose it as a rest from life's sufferings.

[126] The wise man neither spurns living nor does he fear not living. The thought of living does not upset him, nor does he feel that not living is evil. And even as one chooses the more pleasant portion of food rather than merely the larger portion, so the wise man seeks to enjoy the most pleasant time of life and not merely the longest time.

The one who exhorts the young to live well and the old to make a good end is foolish, not merely because of the desirability of life, but because the same practice at once teaches one to live well and to die well.

Much worse is the man who says that it is a good thing not to be born. Yet when born, he says, it is "best to pass quickly through the gates of Hades."[3] [127] If he is truly persuaded by what he says, then why does he not make his exit from life? It is an easy thing for him to do if he is firmly resolved.[4] On the other hand, if he is only joking, then he is a thoughtless man among those who do not welcome him.

We should remember that the future is neither wholly ours nor wholly not ours. Accordingly, we must neither count on it as certain to come nor despair of it as certain not to come.

The Different Desires & Pleasure and Pain

We must consider that of the desires, some are natural, and some are groundless.

Of the natural desires, some are necessary, and some are merely natural.

And of the necessary desires, some are necessary for happiness, some for freeing the body from disturbance, and some for living itself.

[128] He who has a firm understanding of these things knows how to direct every choice and every avoidance toward securing bodily health and mental tranquility since this is the goal of a blessedly happy life. Everything we do is for the sake of being free from pain and from fear. The soul's storm scatters as soon as we achieve this condition. Then we have no need to go around looking for anything that is lacking or seeking something else by which the good of the soul and the good of the body will be fulfilled.

We have the need for pleasure only when we feel pain due to the absence of pleasure. When we feel no pain, however, there is no need for pleasure. For this reason, we say that pleasure is the beginning point and goal of living happily. [129] We recognize that pleasure is our first good, present at birth, and that it is the beginning point of every choice and avoidance. We resort to pleasure when we use feeling as the measure for judging every good.

Even though pleasure is our first and inborn good, we nevertheless do not choose every pleasure. Rather, we oftentimes forgo many pleasures when a greater annoyance will follow from choosing them. And oftentimes we acknowledge that many pains are better than many pleasures when an even greater pleasure follows from patiently enduring these pains for a long period of time. And so, even though every pleasure is naturally good and fitting, not every pleasure is to be chosen. In the same way, even though every pain is bad, not every pain is always to be avoided. [130] To be sure, we may aptly judge every case by measuring one feeling in comparison with the other and taking a look at the advantages and disadvantages of both sides. Sometimes we treat a good thing as though it is bad. On the other hand, sometimes we treat a bad thing as though it is good.

We regard self-sufficiency as a great good. This is not so that we may enjoy just a little in every case, but so that when things are scarce, we may nevertheless be satisfied with little, genuinely persuaded that the ones who derive the greatest pleasure from luxury are the ones who need it the least, and that everything natural is easy to get, but whatever is groundless is hard.

Simple food gives just as much pleasure as rich food does as soon as the hunger pains are gone. [131] A barley cake and water offer the highest possible pleasure when they are given to a hungry man. Getting used to simple and inexpensive food, therefore, aids the health of a man and enables him to perform the necessary requirements of life with resolution. Not only that, but such a habit better disposes us for when we encounter extravagant fare now and again, and makes us fearless in the face of fortune.

So then, when we say that pleasure is the beginning point and goal of life, we do not mean the pleasures of decadent men or the pleasures of sensuality, as some ignorant persons believe, or those who do not agree with us, or those who have willfully misrepresented our position. Rather, by pleasure we mean the absence of pain in the body and of trouble in the soul. [132] A pleasant life is not produced by stringing together one drinking party after another, or by having sex with young boys or women, or by enjoying fish and other delicacies set on a luxurious table. Instead, it is produced by sober reasoning that examines what is responsible for every choice and avoidance, and expels those beliefs by which the greatest confusion lays hold of the soul.

Practical Wisdom and the Wise Man

Practical wisdom is the foundation of all of these things and the greatest good. For this reason, we value practical wisdom even more than philosophy. Every other virtue is produced from practical wisdom, teaching us that we cannot live pleasantly without living wisely, nobly, and justly—just as we cannot live wisely, nobly, and justly without living pleasantly. The virtues have become one with living pleasantly. Living pleasantly is inseparable from the virtues.

[133] Getting this point, who do you believe is better than the man who holds pious beliefs about the gods?—or the one who is altogether free from the fear of death?—or the one who has considered the natural goal of life and understands how easily the limit of good things can be reached and attained, and how the limit of bad things is either short in its duration or slight in its distress?

This man scorns the notion of destiny that some introduce as the master of all things, affirming rather that some things happen by necessity, others by chance, and others through our own agency. This is because he sees that necessity promotes irresponsibility and that chance or fortune is unstable, whereas our own actions are free, and it is to them that praise and blame are attached. [134] It would be better, in fact, to accept the myths told about the gods than to bow beneath the yoke of destiny that the natural philosophers have imposed. The one holds out some small hope that we may escape if we honor the gods, while the other offers inexorable necessity.

Nor does he hold chance (or luck or fortune) to be a god as the many do, assuming as he does that, with a god, nothing is done in a disorderly fashion. Nor does he hold that chance is even an unreliable cause, for he believes that chance delivers nothing good or bad to humans toward living happily—though, to be sure, chance furnishes the beginning point of the excessive goods of fortune and misfortune.

[135] He believes that the bad luck of the thoughtful, reasoning man is better than the good luck of the thoughtless, unreasoning man. In short, in human affairs, it is better for a well-judged effort to fail than for one poorly judged to succeed by means of chance.

FINAL EXHORTATION

Take thought of and practice these matters and related precepts day and night, both by yourself and with others who are like-minded. If you do, then you will never be disturbed by confusion, whether you are awake or dreaming. Instead, you will live like a god among human beings. For the man who lives among immortal blessings loses every likeness to mortal beings.

DIOGENES LAERTIUS: In other works, Epicurus rejects everything having to do with prophecy and divination, as he does in the short epitome, where he says, "The art of divination is unreal, and if it were real, we must suppose what it predicts is nothing to us."

Such are his views on human life—though he has spoken about them more fully elsewhere.

NOTES

[1] For the missing sections (parts of 10.117-121), see the next chapter on the wise man, his nature and activity.

[2] By "the commonly held understanding of the god, the common epithet in writing," we should understand the view of the gods and divine nature that came primarily from Homer and Hesiod. On this, the Greek historian Herodotus (fifth century BC) provides the key witness. In the *Histories*, he explains that the Greeks "did not know until yesterday or the day before, so to speak" much about the gods. They didn't know "when and from where each of the gods came to be, or whether they all had always been, and how they appeared in form." So it was, he testifies, that "Hesiod and Homer . . . taught the Greeks the descent of the gods, and gave the gods their names, and determined their spheres and functions, and described their outward forms" (2.53).

According to Homer and Hesiod, the gods have a few key attributes that outline or define their nature, distinguishing them from human beings. First, the gods are immortal (*athanatos*) and ageless (*agēraos*) (see, for instance, *Iliad* 8.539 and *Odyssey* 5.218). In other words, as Epicurus has it, the gods are indestructible or incorruptible (*aphthartos*). As Hesiod puts it, "The holy race of the immortals always is. They live on forever" (*Theogony* 21). Second, the gods are counted blessed (*makar*). They live a life of ease. In the *Iliad*, Achilles says "the gods . . . live without any sorrow or grief. Their life is a life without care" (24.526). In the *Odyssey*, Homer reveals that "upon Olympus the blessed gods are delighted every day" (6.46). Finally, the gods or divine beings are different from human beings. In the *Iliad*, the god Apollo makes the point to the Greek hero Diomedes in this way: "Consider what I have to say, son of Tydeus, and fall back. You

shouldn't think of yourself as equal to the gods. You're not. The immortal gods and men who walk the earth are not the same kind of tribe or being" (5.440-442).
[3] See, for instance, Theognis of Megara 425-428: "Not to be born and not to look upon the bright light of the sun—this is the best of all for mortal men upon the earth. But to lie dead beneath a huge pile of dirt and to pass through the gates of Hades—this is the best when a man is already born."
[4] Regarding suicide, which he *does not* recommend, Epicurus elsewhere declares, "That man is small in every way who has many good reasons to commit suicide" (*Vatican Sayings* 38). Otherwise he states, "The wise man will not withdraw from life—even when he has lost sight" (Diogenes Laertius, *Lives* 10.119).

For Epicurus, the general pleasure of living is always greater than and so outweighs the general or even specific pain(s) of life *if we are living well*. See, for instance, what L. Manlius Torquatus says: ". . . There is no moment when the pleasures he experiences do not outweigh the pains." And: ". . . Pains are never so severe that the anguish is more than the joy" (in Cicero, *On the Ends* 1.62). This does not mean that pain is entirely absent for the one who is happy or living well or tranquilly. It is just that, if we pay close attention, the balance is always in favor of pleasure, an overall sense of well-being.

The big question, therefore, is: are we living well? Which is to ask: are we listening to the voice of practical wisdom? Are we living virtuously (wisely, nobly, justly, moderately, courageously)? Are we living oriented to friendship? Are we living simply?—for what truly matters? Or are we living for what is unnecessary and groundless or empty?—things like money or reputation (fame, honor, glory) or a great quantity and variety of pleasure (rather than that pleasure which adheres to the "measure of pleasure," which is the simple absence of pain)?

For Epicureanism, the goal is to know the simple joy (*chara*) of life—of *being*—rather than complexities that are far from certain; it is to be at peace, to experience tranquility (*ataraxia*).

Suicide is not the solution to the problem of living. Rather, time is, which is to say that living another minute, hour, day, or week is the way to go. And if we need to, we will live with the help of other human beings—a priest or minister, a counselor or psychiatrist, a wise friend, relative, or mentor.

By the way, if these remarks seem to go beyond Epicurus or seem inappropriate in an "academic" presentation of his work, we at the Cave counter by highlighting the fact that we do not read Epicurus or others for mere academic reasons but in order to practice, as our mission statement says, to apply ancient wisdom to our contemporary ways and lives.

THE WISE MAN[1]

HIS NATURE & ACTIVITY

IN BRIEF: *Diogenes Laertius explores the views of Epicurus on the nature and activity of the wise man in terms of the wise man's origin and disposition; his experience and expression of various feelings and emotions; his stance toward friends and slaves, as well as love, marriage, and sex; his participation in city politics and public speaking; his attitude to those in power; his involvement with business affairs and moneymaking; his approach to maintaining reputation; his involvement with setting up a school and literary discussions; his writings; the nature of his views; as well as other points regarding the wise man.*

DIOGENES LAERTIUS writes:

LET US GO through the views of Epicurus and his school regarding the wise man.

Harm arises among men through hatred, envy, and contempt. The wise man skirts these by means of reason.

Once a man has become wise, he will not assume the opposite disposition—not of his own free will, anyway.

The wise man will be more affected by feelings, but this will not hinder his wisdom.

The wise man cannot come into existence in every bodily condition or among every people group.

[118] The wise man is happy even when he is twisted on the rack. . . . Even so, he will give vent to cries and groans.[2]

The wise man alone will feel gratitude toward friends—those present and absent alike. He will show it by word and deed.

As for mixing with women in love, the wise man will submit to the restrictions imposed by the law—so Diogenes says in his epitome of Epicurus' ethical teachings.

The wise man will not punish his household slaves; rather, he will show mercy to them and grant forgiveness to any who are earnest.

Epicureans do not believe a wise man will fall in love. Nor will he worry about his funeral rites. According to them, love does not come by divine inspiration—that is what Diogenes says in the twelfth book.

The wise man will not speak with beautiful flourishes in public.

Epicureans say that sexual intercourse never benefited anyone. One must be content if it has not caused harm.

[119] Furthermore, the wise man will not marry and have children—that is what Epicurus says in the *Problems* and in *On Nature*. Whether he will marry or not depends on the circumstances of his life. Some will turn him away.

In the *Symposium*, Epicurus says that the wise man will not speak or behave foolishly while drinking.

The wise man will not meddle with politics—as stated in the first book of *On Human Life*. Nor will he become a tyrant.

The wise man will not live like a Cynic—or so says the second book of *On Human Life*. Nor will he beg for alms.

He states in the same book that the wise man will not withdraw himself from life—even when he has lost sight.

According to Diogenes in the fifth book of the *Collected Writings*, the wise man will also feel grief.

[120] The wise man will take his case to court.

He will leave writings behind when he dies, but he will not deliver a panegyric in a public assembly.

He will make plans regarding his property and plan for the future.

The wise man will be fond of nature, of the countryside.

The wise man directly takes on chance, face to face.

He never gives up a friend.

The wise man will give thought to a good reputation only so as to avoid being looked down on.

He will enjoy state-sponsored festivals and spectacles more than other men.

He will set up votive images.

He is indifferent to whether he is well-off or not.

The wise man alone will be able to discuss music and poetry well. That said, he will not actually compose poetry.

One wise man is no wiser in what he does than another.

If he is in need, the wise man will make money—but only by means of his wisdom and skill.

When it is appropriate, he will serve the one in power.

The wise man will rejoice with anyone who makes things right.

He will found a school—but not so as to gather a crowd around him. He will give public readings—but only by request.

The wise man will have opinions without being at a loss. (He will not be a mere skeptic.)

He will remain as he is even when he is sleeping.

On occasion, the wise man will die for a friend.

The wise man holds that not all faults are equal.

He believes that health is in some cases good but in other cases an indifferent thing, neither good nor bad.

And that courage does not spring up naturally, but by means of rationally figuring out what is expedient.

And that friendship arises because we are in need. That said, friendship involves sacrifice, just as we have to cast seed into the earth. Friendship is maintained by a partnership in the enjoyment of life's pleasures.

[121] There are two kinds of happiness. There is the happiness of the god, the highest kind, which cannot be increased. The other kind may increase or decrease in terms of pleasures.

NOTES

[1] "Wise man," here, is *sophos*, a word related to the Greek for wisdom, *sophia*.

[2] The Classics Cave has slightly reordered the passage here. The passage actually reads: "The wise man is happy even when he is twisted on the rack. The

wise man alone will feel gratitude toward friends—those present and absent alike. He will show it by word and deed. Even so, he will give vent to cries and groans. As for mixing with women in love . . ."

EPICUREANISM & CYRENAICISM
A BRIEF COMPARISON

IN BRIEF: *Given the evidence of Epicurus' own writing, and that of others, Diogenes Laertius explains some of Epicurus' opinions on pleasure and pain and compares them to Cyrenaic views.*

DIOGENES LAERTIUS writes: [136]

W HEN IT COMES to the nature of pleasure, Epicurus and the Cyrenaics differ.[1] The Cyrenaics only accept kinetic pleasure, that is, pleasure in motion; they do not accept static, or katastematic, pleasure. By contrast, Epicurus accepts both.[2]

He also recognizes both pleasure of the soul and of the body — as he says in his works *On Choice and Avoidance*, and in *On the Goal of Human Life*, and in the first book of his work *On Human Life*, and in his letter to the philosophers in Mytilene.

Diogenes says the same about pleasure in the seventeenth book of his *Collected Writings*. And so too does Metrodorus in his *Timocrates*. His words are, "Pleasure is thought of as both kinetic and katastematic."

In his work *On Choice*, Epicurus says, "Freedom from trouble and freedom from pain are katastematic pleasures. Joy and good cheer are viewed as kinetic and active."

[137] Epicurus further disagrees with the Cyrenaics in this way. They believe that pains of the body are worse than pains of the soul. Their evidence is that wrongdoers are punished with bodily pain. By contrast, Epicurus holds that pains of the soul are worse. His evidence is that flesh suffers whatever distress is at hand, whereas the soul suffers what has already gone by, what is present, and

what is to come. In this way, Epicurus believes that pleasures of the soul are greater than those of the body.

For proof that pleasure is the goal of life, he points to the fact that living things, as soon as they are born, are quite satisfied with pleasure, whereas they are naturally upset with pain—and this without rational reflection. So then, we avoid pain based on our own feelings, even as when Heracles, devoured by the poisoned robe, cries aloud,

> biting and yelling, all around the cliffs resounding,
> both the steep headlands of Locris and the heights of Euboea.[3]

[138] Moreover, we choose the virtues for the sake of pleasure and not on their own account, even as we take medicine for the sake of health. Diogenes also says this in the twentieth book of his *Collected Writings*. He also says that education is a way of life. Epicurus declares that virtue is the only thing that is inseparable from pleasure. Everything else—things like food, for example—may be separated from pleasure.

NOTES

[1] Founded by Aristippus of Cyrene (c. 435-356 BC) and named after his hometown, Cyrenaicism was an ancient Greek philosophy that promoted pleasure as the chief goal of life.

[2] For discussions on the nature of and differences between kinetic and katastematic pleasure, see A.A. Long, *Hellenistic Philosophy: Stoics, Epicureans, Sceptics,* 2nd ed. (London: Duckworth, 1986), 64-65, and J.M. Rist, *Epicurus: An Introduction* (Cambridge: Cambridge University Press, 1972), 170-172. In short, kinetic pleasure is that which accompanies the ongoing act of satisfying some desire, whereas katastematic pleasure is that of being satisfied after the act. For example, when one is thirsty, one drinks water. The ongoing act of quenching thirst is satisfying—pleasing (a kinetic pleasure). When one stops drinking, one is satisfied (no longer thirsty), which is also pleasing (a katastematic pleasure). We might call the former "acting" (or "active") pleasure and the latter "standing" (or "static") pleasure. See "kinetic" and "static" in the Glossary.

[3] Sophocles, *The Women at Trachis* 787-788.

PART 3

THE BEGINNING OF HAPPINESS
THE SAYINGS OF EPICURUS

THE PRINCIPAL TEACHINGS
THE KEY TEACHINGS & SAYINGS OF EPICURUS

IN BRIEF: *Epicurus offers forty teachings about how to live well. These doctrines address the blessed existence of the gods; the insignificance of death; the benefits of studying nature and the good of a reasoned-based life; the three kinds of desire; the nature and limit of pleasure and pain; wealth; the virtues, with an emphasis on justice; security and confidence relative to others; and the great value of friendship.*

DIOGENES LAERTIUS: [138]

L ET US NOW, then, add the finishing stroke to this whole work, as some would say, and to the philosopher Epicurus' life, by citing his *Principal Teachings*, thereby bringing the whole work to a close, and making its end to coincide with the beginning of happiness.

FIVE KEY POINTS FOR LIVING WELL HAVING TO DO WITH THE GODS, DEATH, PLEASURE AND PAIN, AND THE VIRTUES[1]

[139] 1. A blessed and indestructible being is not bothered by troublesome business, nor does this being trouble others. Therefore, such a being is free from anger and the feeling that he is obliged to grant favors since these feelings imply weakness.[2]

2. Death means nothing to us. This is so because the body, when it breaks up into its various elements, has no sensation. And that which has no sensation is nothing to us.

3. The standard measure for the greatest amount of pleasure is the removal of every pain. Whenever pleasure is present, as long as it lasts, there is neither pain nor distress nor both together.

[140] 4. Ongoing pain does not last long in the flesh. Extreme pain is present for a very short time. And mild pain that barely outweighs pleasure in the flesh does not last for many days in a row. Even long-lasting sickness involves more pleasure than pain in the flesh.

5. It is impossible to live pleasantly without living wisely, nobly, and justly—just as it is impossible to live wisely, nobly, and justly without living pleasantly. The person who fails to inaugurate a wise, noble, and just life is the person who does not have a pleasant life.

LIVING CONFIDENTLY AND SECURELY AMONG OTHER MEN

[141] 6. Any means whatsoever of acquiring confidence before other men, and security, is a natural good.

7. Some men desire to be honored and admired, believing that in this way they will secure their own personal safety from other men. They have attained the natural good inasmuch as their lives are secure from danger. If, however, their lives are not secure from danger, they have not obtained that for which they reached out in the beginning in response to the prompting of nature.

PLEASURE—IN TERMS OF QUANTITY AND QUALITY

8. In itself, no pleasure is evil. That said, the things that produce certain pleasures entail annoying troubles many times greater than the pleasures themselves.

[142] 9. If every pleasure were condensed within time and all over the whole human organism—or, at any rate, around the principal parts of a man's nature—then the pleasures would not differ from one another.

10. If things that produce pleasure for decadent humans truly freed them from their fearful thoughts—the fears inspired by things that happen in the sky, and death, and pain—, and if, moreover, these things taught them the limit of their desires, then we would never have any reason to find fault with them since they would then be filled full with pleasures and would never suffer pain, which is the real evil, whether bodily pain or mental distress.

THE BENEFIT OF STUDYING NATURE—
FREEDOM FROM FEAR AND WORRY

11. We would have never needed to investigate natural phenomena if we had not been disturbed by worry about things that happen in the sky or by the misgiving that death means something to us or by our failure to understand the boundary markers of suffering and desire.

[143] 12. It is impossible to set ourselves free from fear regarding the most important things if we do not understand the nature of the whole cosmos, and if we are apprehensive about what the myths tell us. Consequently, without the study of nature, there is no enjoyment of pleasures unmixed with fear and worry.

13. There is no real advantage in acquiring personal safety from other men as long as we are worried about things above or below the earth or in the infinite expanse of things.

VARIOUS TEACHINGS

14. Great power and resources may up to a certain point give us a sense of personal safety relative to other men. In general, however, a sense of personal safety is established upon a quiet life withdrawn from the many.

[144] 15. Natural wealth is both limited and easy to get. But the wealth based on groundless opinion grows without limit.

16. Luck rarely interferes with the wise man. Rather, it is reason that has managed, does manage, and will manage the greatest and most essential things throughout the course of a wise man's life.

17. The just man is least troubled, whereas the unjust man experiences a full measure of the greatest trouble.

THE LIMITS OF HEALTHY PLEASURE AND LIFE

18. Pleasure in the flesh will not increase after need-based pain is removed. After that, pleasure may only be varied. And the limit of pleasure in the mind is reached in thinking about these and like things that used to cause the greatest fears in the mind.

[145] 19. Unlimited time and limited time carry an equal amount of pleasure if we measure the limits of pleasure by reason.

20. While the flesh behaves as though the limits of pleasure are unlimited and thus it would take an unlimited amount of time to furnish these pleasures, the mind—having reasoned out the purpose and limits of the flesh, and having banished fears having to do with eternity—provides a complete life that does not require an unlimited amount of time. Nevertheless, the mind does not avoid pleasure. And even when circumstances cause one to leave life, the mind enjoys the best life.

[146] 21. He who understands the limits of life knows how easy it is to procure what it takes to remove the pain of need and make the whole of life complete. Therefore, there is no need for things that can only be procured by means of struggle and troublesome business.

OBSERVATIONAL AND REASONED-BASED CONCLUSIONS AND BEHAVIOR

22. Regarding the goal of life, it is necessary to take into account what truly exists and all clear evidence to which we refer our opinions. Otherwise, everything will be full of poor judgment and disturbing confusion.

23. If you oppose all sensation, then you will have no means by which to judge even those sensations you declare false.

[147] 24. If you wholly reject any single sensation and do not pause to make a distinction between an opinion based on that which awaits confirmation and that which is already present to sensation or the feelings or presentations in the mind, then you will throw into confusion the remaining sensations by your groundless opinions. Consequently, you will be rejecting every criterion. And if in your opinion-based notions you hastily affirm as true all that awaits confirmation, as well as that which does not, you will not abandon falsehood. Rather, you will maintain complete ambiguity whenever it is a case of determining what is correct and what is incorrect.

[148] 25. If at any moment you do not direct each of your actions to the goal of life indicated by nature, but, instead, you turn aside to some

other goal in the act of pursuing some object or avoiding it, your activity will not be consistent with the conclusions drawn from reason.

UNNECESSARY DESIRES

26. Unnecessary desires are those that lead to no pain if they remain unsatisfied. They involve an appetite that is easily relieved whenever its satisfaction is hard to procure or when it seems likely to cause harm.

THE GREAT VALUE OF FRIENDSHIP

27. Of all the means that are procured by wisdom to ensure blessed happiness throughout the whole of life, by far the most important is the acquisition of friendship.

28. The same judgment that produces the confidence that nothing terrible is eternal or long-lasting also perceives the personal safety that is accomplished by friendship relative to these same time-bound and terrible things.

THE THREE KINDS OF DESIRE

[149] 29. Of the desires, some are natural and necessary, whereas some are natural but unnecessary. Others are neither natural nor necessary but arise thanks to groundless notions.[3]

30. If one's zeal is intense in the case of those natural desires that lead to no pain if they remain unsatisfied, then such desires arise thanks to groundless notions. And when they do not vanish, it is not because of their own nature but thanks to those groundless human notions.

JUSTICE AND INJUSTICE

[150] 31. Natural justice is a pledge of reciprocal advantage neither to harm one another nor to be harmed.

32. Nothing is just or unjust for those animals that are unable to make non-harm agreements—that is, compacts neither to harm one

another nor be harmed. The same is true for those people groups that either are unable or unwilling to make non-harm agreements.

33. There is no such thing as justice in itself. Rather, justice is an agreement neither to harm nor be harmed that is made when men gather together from time to time in various places.

[151] 34. Injustice is not something evil in itself. Rather the evil coincides with the worry and worming fear that one will not escape the notice of those who are responsible for punishing injustice.

35. It is impossible for the man who secretly violates the agreement to neither harm one another nor be harmed to feel confident that he will remain undiscovered, even if up to the present moment he has already escaped ten thousand times. No, to the end of his life such a man is never sure he will remain undetected.

36. Taken generally, justice is the same for all because of its reciprocal advantage when men associate with one another. But in its specific application to places and conditions, justice is different depending on the circumstances.

[152] 37. Among the things considered just by custom, whatever is affirmed to be reciprocally advantageous in meeting the needs of men who associate with one another is characterized as just, whether or not it is the same for all. On the other hand, the law or custom that proves not to be reciprocally advantageous when men associate no longer possesses a just nature. And even if what was considered the just reciprocal advantage changes after having been considered just for some time, it is nonetheless true that it was really just for that period of time—as long as we do not trouble ourselves with groundless discourses, but simply look at the facts.

[153] 38. If circumstances have not changed, and things considered just by custom are shown not to correspond with the preconception of justice in terms of the results, then these things are not just. And if circumstances do change, and the things considered just turn out to be no longer advantageous, then those things were just for a time relative to the advantages of men associating with one another as fellow citizens, but later on, as soon as there was no advantage, they were no longer just.

CONFIDENCE AND SECURITY

[154] 39. The man who best endures the lack of confidence relative to things external to himself is the man who assimilates to himself what he is able. At the very least he does not alienate those things he is unable to assimilate. Nevertheless, when he is unable to do even this, he avoids all connection with these external things, banishing them to the extent that is profitable.

40. The ones who are able to establish the greatest security relative to those who live around them are the ones able to live pleasantly among others thanks to this firm guarantee of security. And after enjoying the relationship to the full, they do not piteously lament its completion when it ends.

NOTES

[1] This and the following subtitles are not found in the original Greek. They are provided by the Cave for the sake of organization and to facilitate memory.

[2] Added commentary: "In another place he says that the gods are discernible by reason alone, some being numerically distinct, while others result uniformly from the continuous influx of similar images directed to the same spot and in human form."

[3] Added commentary: "Epicurus regards as natural and necessary desires that bring relief from pain, such as drink when we are thirsty. And by desires that are natural and unnecessary he means those that merely vary the pleasure without removing the pain, such as costly food. And by desires that are neither natural nor necessary he means those for crowns and the erection of statues in one's honor."

THE VATICAN SAYINGS[1]
MORE KEY TEACHINGS & SAYINGS OF EPICURUS

IN BRIEF: *Epicurus touches on many subjects in the* Vatican Sayings, *including friendship, dreams, pleasure and pain, the desires, hunger, envy, anger, habits, mortality, necessity, the relative value of customs, the happiness of older people, the love of money, self-sufficiency, tranquility, and the delight of doing philosophy. Epicurus also gives advice related to several aspects of living well, such as always keeping in mind the good that has occurred; the benefit of desiring what one has and what is present; the need to obey nature; the benefit of limits; the good of gratitude; how to endure pain; why one should avoid wrongdoing; and being joyful today. Lastly, Epicurus offers various explanations for phenomena, including why we sometimes choose bad things; the ongoing causes of erotic desire; the relative value of poverty and wealth; and the purpose of studying nature.*

E VERY PAIN IS easy to ignore. Severe pain lasts for a brief time, whereas long-lasting pain in the flesh is not severe (4).[2]

7. While it is hard enough for a wrongdoer to avoid getting caught, it is impossible for him to maintain confidence that he will remain uncaught.

9. Necessity is something bad, but there is no necessity to live by means of necessity.

10. Remember that you are mortal and have a limited amount of time to live. And that you have devoted yourself to discussions on nature for all time and eternity and have seen "things that are now and are to come and have been."

11. For most human beings, being still and quiet is numbness, but being in motion is frenzy.

14. We come into being only once and will not be born a second

time. Rather, we necessarily will never exist again—forever. And though you have no power over tomorrow, you put off feeling joy today. Life is consumed by such indecision and procrastination! And so, each one of us is dying without engaging in life today.

15. We value our own customs as special, whether or not they are actually useful or esteemed by other men. In like manner we should value the customs of our neighbors if they are reasonable.

16. No one who sees something bad chooses it for itself; rather, enticed by it as something good relative to something even worse, he goes after it.

17. It is not the young man that we consider most happy, but the old man who has lived well. Even though the young man is in his prime, he drifts, confused and many-minded thanks to the fortunes of happenstance, whereas the old man has passed into old age even as a ship sails into a harbor, secure in gratitude for the good things that earlier he did not even hope for.

18. When the opportunity to see and be and live with the other is taken away, then the erotic passion vanishes.

19. He who fails to remember the good that existed yesterday becomes an old man today.

21. We must obey nature rather than doing violence to her. We will obey nature by satisfying the necessary desires and the natural desires, too, as long as they do no harm, but sharply rejecting the harmful desires.

23. Every friendship is desirable in itself, even though it begins because of its utility.

24. Dreams have neither a divine nature nor a prophetic power; rather, they arise following the impact of images.

25. When measured by the goals of nature, poverty is great wealth. And wealth is great poverty if it is not limited.

26. One must grasp that both the long and the short speech lead to the same end.

27. While the benefit of other pursuits only comes upon completion, in doing philosophy, delight coincides with the investigation— since enjoyment does not arise after learning, but learning and enjoyment appear together.

28. Neither approve those who grasp after friendship nor those who shrink from it. But one must risk delight for the delight of friendship.

29. Speaking honestly, when I discourse about nature, I would rather deliver oracles proclaiming what is useful for all human beings, even if no one understands me, than agree with common opinion and enjoy the ongoing praise offered by many.

30. Some men spend their whole lives procuring for themselves those things necessary for life without grasping that each of us was poured a mortal mixture to drink at our birth.

31. We may possibly provide security against other dangers, but when it comes to death, we men all live in a city without walls.

32. Reverence for a wise man is a great good for the reverent man.

33. The flesh cries out, "No hunger! No thirst! No freezing cold!" Whoever confidently has what it takes to satisfy these desires may rival even Zeus for happiness.

34. Our need is not so much for the advantage that comes from our friends as it is for the confidence that comes from that advantage.

35. You must not ruin what is present by a longing for what is absent; rather, keep in mind that these things were what you previously desired.

37. Nature is feeble and sick when faced with something bad rather than with something good. This is so because pleasure preserves nature whole, whereas pain breaks it down.

38. That man is small in every way who has many good reasons to commit suicide.

39. The true friend is neither the one who always seeks some advantage, nor is he the one who never links advantage with friendship. The one trades goodwill for compensation, while the other cuts off hope for the future.

40. One who states that everything happens by necessity has no case against another who declares that nothing happens by necessity since even that claim happens by necessity.

41. At one and the same time, we must laugh and do philosophy and manage our households and the rest of our private affairs, always proclaiming the sayings of the true philosophy.

42. The same moment includes both the beginning of the greatest good and deliverance from what is bad.

43. While it is unholy to love money that has been unjustly won, it is shameful to love it if it is justly won since it is unbecoming to be stingy even with the support of justice.

44. The wise man who has measured himself with necessary things knows better how to give than to take, so large a treasury of self-sufficiency has he found.

45. The study of nature does not produce boastful men or bigmouths or those who show off the learning that the many argue about; rather, it produces fearless and self-sufficient men, who pride themselves on their own personal goods rather than on circumstances.

46. Let us completely get rid of thoughtless habits, even as we would worthless men who have done us great harm for a long time.

47. I have anticipated you, Fortune, and have strengthened myself for all your attacks. We will neither surrender ourselves to you nor to any other circumstance. But when it is time for us to go, we will depart from life, having no regard for it and for those who vainly cling to it, and proclaiming aloud in a beautiful song that we have lived well.

48. So long as we are on the road of life, we should try to make the latter part of the journey better than the former. And whenever we arrive at the end, we should equally enjoy ourselves.

51. I hear from you that the abundant stirring of the flesh disposes you to the pleasures of sex. Follow your inclination as you wish, provided only that you neither violate the laws, nor disturb well-established customs, nor harm any of your neighbors, nor injure your own flesh, nor waste your possessions. Even so, you cannot avoid being checked by one of these barriers. A man never gets any good from sexual pleasure; rather, he is content if he is not harmed.

52. Friendship dances around the world of men calling out to all of us, "Rise up to happiness!"

53. We must envy no one. For good men do not deserve envy, and the more worthless men succeed, the more they bring ruin upon themselves.

54. We must not merely pretend to practice philosophy; rather, we

must actually do it. For we do not merely need the appearance of health, but true health.

55. We must cure misfortune with gratitude for what has been lost and with the knowledge that it is impossible to undo what has happened.

56-57. The wise man feels no more pain when he is stretched on the rack than when his friend is tortured in such a manner. And he would die for his friend. For if he betrays his friend, then his whole life will be troubled and disturbed by a lack of confidence in friendship.

58. We must free ourselves from the prison house of those public services required every year and other political affairs.

59. The belly is not insatiable as the many declare. Instead, the opinion that the belly's satisfaction is without limits is false.

60. Every man leaves life as though he had just been born.

61. The appearance of one's neighbors is happiest when the first encounter produces harmony or at least a zeal for harmonious relations.

62. If parents need to get angry with their offspring, it is surely disrespectful for their children to resist their wrath and foolish for them not to beg forgiveness. On the other hand, if there is no need for their wrath, but the anger is without reason, then it is absurd for the child to exacerbate their irrational behavior by hanging on to his own animosity and by not seeking to win them over by other means.

63. There is a purity in the minimum. The thoughtless man resembles someone who suffers from a lack of limits.

64. The approval of others is necessarily their own business. As for us, we must get on with our own healing.

65. It is impious for a man to beg the gods for what he is able to supply himself.

66. We sympathize with our friends not by wailing in lamentation but by thoughtful reflection.

67. It is not possible for a man living a free life to amass a lot of money and possessions since this is no easy accomplishment without being servile to the masses or those in power. And yet such a free life has acquired everything in ongoing abundance. But if by chance he does

acquire a lot of money and possessions, he will easily distribute these to acquire the good will of those around him.

68. Nothing is enough for someone for whom enough is very little.

69. The ingratitude of the soul makes the living being greedy for an endless variation in its way of life.

70. Do nothing in your life that will cause you fear if discovered by your neighbor.

71. We must present the following questions to all our desires. What will happen to me if the desire I wish to satisfy is fulfilled? What will happen if it is not?

73. Some bodily pains are useful as a safeguard against the occurrence of similar bodily pains.

74. In a philosophical debate, he who loses wins more because he has learned something.

75. The saying, "Look to the end of a long life," shows ingratitude for past good fortune.

76. Growing old, you are the sort of man I would recommend. You know the difference between doing philosophy for yourself and for the sake of Greece. I rejoice with you.

77. The greatest fruit of self-sufficiency is freedom.

78. The noble man is most engaged with wisdom and friendship. Of these, the one is a mortal good, but the other is immortal.

79. The man who is free from disturbance within himself is no trouble to another man.

80. A young man's share in salvation comes from watching over his own age and guarding against whatever will wreck everything through raging desires.

81. Soul-disturbance is not resolved, nor is true joy produced, by the possession of the greatest wealth, nor by the honor and admiration of the many, nor by any other thing that is the result of indefinite factors.

NOTES

[1] The collection of Epicurus' teachings and sayings known as the *Vatican Sayings* is from a fourteenth century manuscript tucked away in the Vatican Library. Some of the sayings (here omitted) are the same as the *Principal Teachings*

found in Diogenes Laertius, *Lives* 10.139-154. These include the following (the *Principal Teachings* number is placed in parentheses): 1(1), 2(2), 3(4), 5(5), 6(35), 8(15), 12(17), 13(37), 20(29), 22(19), 49(12), 50(8), 72(13). Another saying (number 36) is about Epicurus and thus, as scholars recognize, not by him; it is also omitted.

[2] For reasons having to do with parallel formatting, we have placed the number of this saying in parentheses at the end of the saying. To be clear, this is *Vatican Sayings* 4.

PART 4

EPICURUS
THE MAN HIMSELF

THE LIFE OF EPICURUS
HIS BIRTH, LIFE, DEATH & SCHOOL

IN BRIEF: *Utilizing various sources, Diogenes Laertius reports the basics of Epicurus' life—the when and where of his birth, life, and death, as well as the organization and continuation of Epicurus' school of philosophy.*

DIOGENES LAERTIUS: [1]

IN HIS BOOK *On Noble Birth*, Metrodorus reports that Epicurus, the son of Neocles and Chaerestrate, was from Athens. Within Athens, he was from the deme of Gargettus. He also says that he was from the family of the Philaidae.

Some others, including Heraclides in his *Epitome* of Sotion, declare that Epicurus was raised in Samos after the Athenians had sent settlers there. He later came to Athens at the age of eighteen, at the time when Xenocrates was lecturing at the Academy, and Aristotle in Chalcis.

Upon the death of Alexander of Macedon and the expulsion of the Athenian settlers from Samos by Perdiccas, Epicurus left Athens to join his father in Colophon. He spent some time there collecting students before returning to Athens later on in the archonship of Anaxicrates. There he spent time with some others studying philosophy. Subsequently, he put forward his own unique views and organized the school that is named after him. . . .

[10] Though Epicurus lived when very difficult times prevailed in his homeland, he nevertheless passed his life in Greece. That said, he did sail across the sea to Ionia two or three times in order to visit his friends there.

As for his friends, they came to him from all parts and lived with him in his Garden, as Apollodorus affirms. . . .

[14] In his *Chronology*, Apollodorus reports that Epicurus was born in the third year of the 109th Olympiad, in the archonship of Sosigenes, on the seventh day of the month of Gamelion, in the seventh year after the death of Plato.

[15] When he was thirty-two, Epicurus organized and ran a school for five years in Mytilene and Lampsacus. He then moved to Athens.

Epicurus died in Athens in the second year of the 127th Olympiad, in the archonship of Pytharatus. He was seventy-two. Hermarchus, the son of Agemortus, a Mytilenian man, took over the school.

In his letters, Hermarchus states that Epicurus died thanks to stones that blocked the flow of his urine. He suffered this malady for fourteen days. Hermippus relates that he entered a bronze bath of warm water and asked for wine unmixed with water, which he drank to the last. [16] After this, having already encouraged his friends to keep his teachings in mind, he died.

Here is something of my own about Epicurus:

"Farewell, my friends. Keep in mind my teachings." Such were Epicurus' last words before he died. He stepped into a warm bath and drank unmixed wine. His next drink was in cold Hades.

Such was the life of the man Epicurus, and such was his death.

THE TURN TO PHILOSOPHY
EPICURUS' TEACHERS & STUDY OF PHILOSOPHY

IN BRIEF: *Diogenes Laertius offers various reports on how Epicurus came to study philosophy, with whom, and when Epicurus developed his own views and started his own school.*

DIOGENES LAERTIUS: [2]

U PON THE DEATH of Alexander of Macedon and the expulsion of the Athenian settlers from Samos by Perdiccas, Epicurus left Athens to join his father in Colophon. He spent some time there collecting students before returning to Athens later on in the archonship of Anaxicrates.

There he spent time with some others studying philosophy. Subsequently, he put forward his own unique views and organized the school that is named after him.

Epicurus himself declares that he came into contact with philosophy at the age of fourteen. In his first book of his *Life of Epicurus*, Apollodorus the Epicurean explains that he turned to philosophy thanks to his contempt for teachers who were unable to explain the meaning of *chaos* found in Hesiod.

According to Hermippus, however, Epicurus himself began his career as a teacher. Nevertheless, when he happened to encounter the works of Democritus, he took up philosophy. [3] This is the point of Timon's allusion in the following lines:

> The last and most shameless of all the natural philosophers, who came from Samos, a teacher and the son of a teacher. He himself was one of the most unmanageable of living beings.

According to Philodemus the Epicurean in the tenth book of his comprehensive work *On the Philosophers*, Epicurus' three brothers, Neocles, Chaeredemus, and Aristobulus, joined him in his study of philosophy thanks to Epicurus' own urging. His slave named Mys also joined him—according to Myronianus' report in his *Historical Parallels*. . . .

[12] Diocles reports that, among the ancient philosophers, Epicurus favored Anaxagoras the most, though he occasionally disagreed with him. He also favored Archelaus, Socrates' teacher. Diocles adds that he used to train his students in committing his treatises to memory.

[13] In his *Chronology*, Apollodorus reports that Epicurus was the student of Nausiphanes and Praxiphanes. But in his letter to Eurylochus, Epicurus himself denies this, saying that he was self-taught.

Both Epicurus and Hermarchus deny the very existence of Leucippus the philosopher. That said, others, including Apollodorus the Epicurean, report that Leucippus was Democritus' teacher. Demetrius the Magnesian affirms that Epicurus also listened to the lectures of Xenocrates. . . .

[14] In his *Life of Epicurus*, Ariston reports that Epicurus' treatise called *The Canon* originated from the *Tripod* of Nausiphanes, adding that Epicurus had been a student of this man, as well as of the Platonist Pamphilus in Samos. He further says that Epicurus began to study philosophy when he was twelve years old, and that he started his own school when he was thirty-two.

SIMPLICITY OF LIFE
PLAIN FOOD & DRINK AMONG FRIENDS

IN BRIEF: *Diogenes Laertius describes the simple Epicurean life in the Garden of Epicurus, one spent in friendship and content with plain bread and water and, perhaps, a small cup of wine.*

DIOGENES LAERTIUS: [10]

E PICURUS' FRIENDS CAME to him from all parts and lived with him in his Garden, as Apollodorus affirms. He also reports that Epicurus purchased the Garden for eighty minae.

[11] And Diocles, in the third book of his *Epitome*, speaks of them as living a quite simple and frugal life. Anyway, they were, he says, content with a cup of poor wine. Otherwise, they were water drinkers.

Diocles also declares that Epicurus did not think that their property should be held in common, as required by the saying of Pythagoras about the shared good of friends. In his view, such a practice implied mistrust. And without trust, there is no friendship.

In his own letters, Epicurus declares that he was content with inexpensive bread and water alone. In one, he says, "Send me a small earthen pot of cheese so that, when I wish, I may feast luxuriously." This was the man who taught that pleasure is the goal of life.

And here is the epigram in which Athenaeus commemorates him [12]:

O men! You weary yourselves with toil for inferior things, insatiably beginning quarrels and battles for gain. And yet the wealth of nature is held to small and humble limits, whereas groundless judgments suggest unlimited growth. Neocles' wise son heard this message from the Muses or from the sacred tripod at Delphi.

EPICURUS' GOODWILL
THE EVIDENCE

IN BRIEF: *Diogenes Laertius recounts evidence indicating Epicurus' goodwill to others—the honor given to him by his city, the loyalty of his friends and students, the ongoing existence of his school, his gratitude and generosity, and his love for the gods and his homeland.*

DIOGENES LAERTIUS: [9]

THE PEOPLE WHO criticize Epicurus are madmen. I say this because there is an abundance of witnesses who attest to his unsurpassed goodwill and kindness to all men.

His homeland, for example, honored him with bronze statues. Moreover, his friends were so many in number that they could hardly be measured by whole cities. No one familiar with the siren charms of his teachings ever deserted him, except for Metrodorus of Stratonicea, who went over to Carneades.[1] Perhaps he was unable to endure the kindness and goodness of Epicurus without feeling some kind of distress.

While nearly every other school has died out, the Epicurean school continues forever without interruption through countless reigns of one scholarch after another.

[10] His gratitude to his parents also attests to his goodwill, as well as his generosity to his brothers, and his kindness to his household slaves. The latter is clear from his will and from the fact that they joined with him in studying philosophy. The most notable of his slaves was Mys, whom I mentioned before. In general, we may point to Epicurus' love for all humankind.

As for the gods and his homeland, it is impossible to describe his piety toward the former and his affection for the latter, yet from an excessive sense of fairness, Epicurus did not engage in the political business of the city.

NOTES

[1] Carneades of Cyrene (c. 214-129 BC) was the founder and head of the New Academy.

THE WRITINGS
STYLE, QUANTITY, QUALITY & TITLES

IN BRIEF: *Diogenes Laertius first comments on Epicurus' writing style before reporting on the number and nature of his writings. He finishes by listing forty-one of the some three hundred rolls or scrolls.*

DIOGENES LAERTIUS: [13]

THE TERMS EPICURUS used for things were ordinary terms. Aristophanes the grammarian credits him with a very characteristic style. Epicurus was so lucid a writer that in the work *On Rhetoric* he makes clarity the only requirement.

[14] And in his letters he replaces the usual greeting, "May you be glad," with "May you do well" and "May you live earnestly." . . .

[26] Epicurus was a most prolific author. He eclipsed everyone who came before him in terms of the number of his writings. These amount to about three hundred rolls, and they do not contain a single citation from other authors. Rather, it is Epicurus himself who speaks throughout.

According to Carneades, the Stoic Chrysippus tried to outdo him in authorship. Carneades calls him the literary parasite of Epicurus. For if the latter ever wrote anything on a topic, then Chrysippus, in his contentiousness, had to write something of equal length. [27] Consequently, he has frequently repeated himself and set down the first thought that occurred to him. And in his haste, he has left things unrevised. And he has so many citations that they alone fill his books—something that is also found in Zeno and Aristotle.

Such, then, is the number and length of Epicurus' writings. The best are as follows:

- *On Nature*—thirty-seven books
- *On Atoms and Void*
- *On Desire*
- *Epitome of Objections to the Natural Philosophers*
- One book addressed to the Megarians
- *Problems*
- *Principal Teachings*
- *On Choice and Avoidance*
- *On the Goal of Human Life*
- *On the Criterion, or the Canon*
- The *Chaeredemus*
- *On the Gods*
- *On Piety*
- [28] The *Hegesianax*
- *On Human Life*—four books
- *On Just and Honest Dealing*
- The *Neocles*—addressed to Themista
- The *Symposium*
- The *Eurylochus*—addressed to Metrodorus
- *On Vision*
- *On the Angle in the Atom*
- *On the Sense of Touch*
- *On Destiny*
- *Teachings on the Feelings*—addressed to Timocrates
- *Discovery of the Future*
- *Exhortations*
- *On Images*
- *On Presentations*
- *Aristobulus*
- *On Music*
- *On Justice and Other Virtues*
- *On Gifts and Gratitude*
- The *Polymedes*
- The *Timocrates*—three books
- The *Metrodorus*—five books
- The *Antidorus*—two books
- *Teachings about Disease*—addressed to Mithras
- The *Callistolas*
- *On Kingship*
- The *Anaximenes*
- The *Letters of Epicurus*.

THE FOLLOWERS
EPICURUS' STUDENTS & SUCCESSORS

IN BRIEF: *Diogenes Laertius relates the most significant of Epicurus' followers as well as some of their written work. Of them, the most notable were Metrodorus, Polyaenus, and Hermarchus, Epicurus' successor, as well as others.*

DIOGENES LAERTIUS: [22]

E PICURUS HAD MANY students and followers. The following were notable:

There was Metrodorus, the son of Athenaeus (or of Timocrates) and of Sande, a citizen of Lampsacus. From his first acquaintance with Epicurus onward, Metrodorus never left him, except for one time when he went home for six months, after which he returned to him. [23] As Epicurus testifies in the introductions to his writings and in the third book of the *Timocrates*, Metrodorus was good in every way. He was so noble that he gave his sister Batis in marriage to Idomeneus, and he himself took Leontion, the Athenian prostitute, as his mistress.

Metrodorus was undaunted in the face of distress and death, as Epicurus declares in the first book of the *Metrodorus*. We learn that he died seven years before Epicurus, in his fifty-third year. In his will that was already cited,[1] Epicurus himself clearly speaks of him as departed and charges his executors to make provision for Metrodorus' children. Metrodorus' brother Timocrates was also his student. But he was a hasty man.[2]

[24] Metrodorus wrote the following works:

- Three books addressed to the physicians
- *On Sensations*
- One book addressed to Timocrates
- *On Magnanimity*
- *On Epicurus' Poor State of Health*
- One book addressed to the dialecticians
- Nine books addressed to the sophists
- *On the Journey to Wisdom*
- *On Change*
- *On Wealth*
- One book addressed to Democritus
- *On Noble Birth.*

There was also Polyaenus, the son of Athenodorus, a citizen of Lampsacus. He was a gentle and friendly man, as Philodemus and his students affirm.

There was also Epicurus' successor Hermarchus, the son of Agemortus, a citizen of Mytilene. Even though Hermarchus was the son of a poor man, he nevertheless devoted himself to rhetoric from an early age. There are in circulation the following exceptionally fine works by him:

- [25] Twenty-two letters on Empedocles
- *On Mathematics*
- One book addressed to Plato
- One book addressed to Aristotle.

Hermarchus died of a disabling of the nerves, which is to say, paralysis. He was a man fully equal to what had happened.

Similarly, there were also Leonteus of Lampsacus and his wife Themista, to whom Epicurus wrote.

Further, there were Colotes and Idomeneus, who were also from Lampsacus.

All these were notable.

And among them there was also Polystratus, the successor of Hermarchus. He was succeeded by Dionysus, and he by Basilides.

Apollodorus, known as the tyrant of the Garden, who wrote over four hundred works, was also notable. And there were the two Ptolemies of Alexandria, the one black and the other white. And there was Zeno of Sidon, the disciple of Apollodorus, a voluminous writer. [26] And Demetrius, who was called the Lacedaemonian. And Diogenes of Tarsus, who wrote the *Select Lectures*.

There were also Orion and others. But genuine Epicureans disparagingly call these men sophists.

NOTES

[1] For Epicurus' will, see Chapter Sixteen. "Already cited" refers to Diogenes Laertius' original presentation of the material related to Epicurus.

[2] For more on Timocrates, the brother of Metrodorus, see Diogenes Laertius, *Lives* 6.

EPICURUS' WILL

WEALTH, BENEFICIARIES & FUTURE ACTIVITIES

IN BRIEF: *Epicurus' will establishes what will happen to his property and possessions, including the Garden and his books, after he dies. He names various beneficiaries, fellow philosophers and their children, and determines how part of his wealth will be utilized. Lastly, he frees his slaves, including Mys, who joined him in the study of philosophy.*

DIOGENES LAERTIUS: [16] Epicurus' last will was as follows:

ACCORDING TO THIS, my will, I give all my property and possessions to Amynomachus, the son of Philocrates, of the deme of Bate, and to Timocrates, the son of Demetrius, of the deme of Potamus.[1]

These gifts shall go to each man in the way indicated by the gift-deed that is deposited in the temple of the Mother goddess [17] on the condition that they will make my Garden and all that is attached to it available to Hermarchus, the son of Agemortus, of Mytilene, and to all those who study philosophy with him, and to those whom Hermarchus may leave as his successors, to live and pursue and practice philosophy.

I also entrust it to all those who practice philosophy according to my teachings that they may, to the best of their ability, maintain the common life that exists in the Garden, together with Amynomachus and Timocrates. And I enjoin their heirs to do the same in the most perfect and secure manner that they can, as well as the successors. Amynomachus and Timocrates shall permit Hermarchus and his companions in philosophy to live in the house in Melite for Hermarchus' lifetime.

[18] Out of the revenues derived from my property, which is here given by me to Amynomachus and Timocrates, I wish that they will, in consultation with Hermarchus, make separate provision for the following: the funeral offerings to my father, mother, and brothers; the customary celebration of my birthday on the tenth day of Gamelion in each year; and for the meeting of all my school held every month on the twentieth day to commemorate Metrodorus and myself according to the rules now in force. They shall also join in celebration of the day commemorating my brothers in the month of Poseidon, and, likewise, the day in the month of Metageitnion that commemorates Polyaenus, as I have done up to now.

[19] Amynomachus and Timocrates shall take care of Epicurus, the son of Metrodorus, and of the son of Polyaenus, for as long as they study philosophy and live with Hermarchus. They shall also provide for the maintenance of Metrodorus' daughter for as long as she is well-behaved and obedient to Hermarchus. And when she comes of age, they shall give her in marriage to a husband selected by Hermarchus from among the members of the school. And out of the revenues accruing to me, Amynomachus and Timocrates shall, in consultation with Hermarchus, give them as much as they judge proper for their maintenance year by year.

[20] They shall make Hermarchus their associate in the management of my revenues, in order that everything may be done with the approval of that man who has grown old with me in the study of philosophy, the one who is left as the head of the school.

Returning to Metrodorus' daughter, when the girl comes of age, Amynomachus and Timocrates shall pay her dowry, taking from the property as much as circumstances allow, subject to the approval of Hermarchus. They shall also provide for Nicanor, even as I have done up to now.

They shall do this so that those members of the school who have rendered service to me in private life, and those who have shown kindness in every way, and those who have chosen to grow old with me in the school, shall never lack the necessities of life—as far as my means may provide.

[21] All my books shall be given to Hermarchus.

And if anything happens to Hermarchus before the children of Metrodorus grow up, then Amynomachus and Timocrates shall give from the funds given by me—as far as possible—enough for their different needs, so long as they are well-behaved.

They shall provide for the rest according to my arrangements, so that everything may be carried out insofar as it is in their power.

Of my slaves, I emancipate Mys, Nicias, and Lycon, and I also give Phaedrium her freedom.

. . .

SUCH WERE THE terms of his will.

NOTES

[1] Do not confuse this Timocrates, an Athenian citizen, with Timocrates, the brother of Metrodorus, who was from Lampsacus.

EPICURUS' FINAL LETTER
THE LETTER TO IDOMENEUS

IN BRIEF: *Epicurus writes to Idomeneus on the last day of his life—a blessed day, he says—explaining what ails him and how he is combatting his sufferings with joyful memories. He finishes with a request for Idomeneus to watch over Metrodorus' children.*

DIOGENES LAERTIUS: [22] And when Epicurus approached the end of his life, he wrote the following letter addressed to Idomeneus:

O N THIS BLESSEDLY happy day, which is also the last day of my life, I write this letter to you.

I both suffer from the fact that I am unable to urinate, and I have been dogged by a dysentery so violent that nothing could possibly add to the excessive nature of my sufferings.

Nevertheless, the joyful condition of my soul, which arises from the recollection of all our discussions, counters all these afflictions.

I ask you to take care of Metrodorus' children in a manner worthy of your life-long attitude to me and to philosophy.

PART 5

EPICUREANISM
AS PRESENTED BY CICERO

EPICUREANISM

IN CICERO'S *ON THE ENDS OF GOOD THINGS AND BAD THINGS*

IN BRIEF: *The Roman L. Manlius Torquatus explains Epicurus' ethical system, namely how pleasure*[1] *is the highest good that leads to a life of tranquility and happiness, and how pain is the opposite. Along the way, he discusses how the virtues produce pleasure and how selfless friendship is central to the Epicurean way of life.*[2]

L. MANLIUS TORQUATUS, THE FRIEND OF CICERO, IS SPEAKING:

WE ARE SEEKING, then, that which is the final and ultimate good, that which all philosophers agree must be of such a nature as to be the end to which all other things are means, while it is not itself a means to anything else.

"Epicurus proposes that this is pleasure, which he holds to be the highest good, while pain is the highest evil. He sets out to prove this in the following manner: [30] every animal, as soon as it is born, longs and strives for pleasure, delighting in it as the highest good, while it rejects pain as the highest evil, driving it away when possible. As long as the animal is not seduced or perverted, it does so thanks to the prompting of nature's own genuine and honest proclamation. Thus, Epicurus refuses to admit any necessity for argument or discussion to *prove* that we seek pleasure and avoid pain. These facts, he thinks, are perceived by the senses, just as fire is perceived to be hot, snow white, and honey sweet. None of these things require an elaborate argument to establish them; it is enough merely to draw attention to them. . . .

"Take away sensation from a human being and nothing remains. It follows that nature herself is the judge of that which is in agreement with or contrary to nature. Aside from pleasure and pain, how does nature perceive or judge a thing in order to seek or avoid something?

[32] ". . . No one rejects, dislikes, or avoids pleasure itself, simply because it is pleasure. Rather, those who do not know how to pursue pleasure rationally encounter consequences that are extremely painful, and so they avoid it. Nor again is there anyone who loves, pursues, or desires to obtain pain itself, simply because it is pain. Rather, it is because at times things happen in which toil and pain can procure some great pleasure. To take a trivial example, which of us ever undertakes laborious physical exercise except to obtain some advantage from it? But who has any right to find fault with a man who chooses to enjoy a pleasure that has no troublesome consequences, or one who avoids a pain that produces no pleasure? [33] On the other hand, we blame with righteous indignation and dislike men who are so charmed and seduced by the allurements of the pleasure of the moment, so blinded by desire, that they cannot foresee the pain and trouble that are bound to follow. And equal blame belongs to those who fail in their duty through weakness of will, which amounts to avoiding toil and pain. These cases are perfectly simple and easy to distinguish. In a free hour, when our power of choice is untrammeled and when nothing prevents our being able to do what we like best, every pleasure is to be received and every pain rejected. But at certain times, and thanks to the claims of duty or the obligations of business, it will often happen that pleasures have to be refused and troubles accepted. In these matters, therefore, the wise man always holds to this principle of selection: he postpones certain pleasures to secure other greater pleasures, or else he endures pains to drive away even worse pains. . . .

[37] ". . . The tendency of all the virtues to produce pleasure is a topic that will be treated in its own place later. At present I will proceed to explain the nature of pleasure itself along with its qualities in order to remove the error of all those who are ignorant in their understanding of our school of philosophy, supposing it to be devoted to pleasure, luxurious and effeminate, when it is serious, moderate, and austere. The pleasure we pursue is not that kind

alone which directly affects our physical nature with a delightful feeling—a positively agreeable perception of the senses. Rather, as we understand it, the greatest pleasure is that which is perceived upon the removal of every pain. When we are delivered from pain, we delight in the liberation itself—in the absence of every trouble and distress. But everything that causes delight is a pleasure—just as everything that is displeasing is a pain. Therefore, the complete removal of pain has correctly been termed a pleasure. For example, when hunger and thirst are banished by food and drink, the mere fact of getting rid of the distress of each causes a consequent pleasure. So, generally, the removal of pain causes pleasure to take its place.

[38] "Accordingly, Epicurus held that there is no such thing as a neutral state of feeling intermediate between pleasure and pain. For the state supposed by some thinkers to be intermediate—characterized as it is by the absence of every pain—is itself, he held, a pleasure. Not only that, but it is truly the highest pleasure. A man who is conscious of his condition at all must necessarily feel pleasure or pain. But Epicurus holds that the absence of every pain defines the highest pleasure. Beyond this, pleasure may be varied and divided, but it may not be enlarged and extended. . . .

[40] "The truth of the position that pleasure is the final good will most readily appear from the following illustration. Let us posit a man living in the continuous enjoyment of numerous and great pleasures in both body and mind, undisturbed either by the presence or prospect of pain. What possible state of existence could we describe as being more excellent or more desirable? One so situated must possess a strength of mind that is a defense against all fear of death or pain. He will know that death is the complete removal of sensation, and that long-term pain is slight and severe pain is brief, so that its intensity is compensated by brief duration and its continuance by diminishing severity. [41] Let such a man, moreover, have no dread of any supernatural power. Let him never allow the pleasures of the past to fade away, but constantly renew their enjoyment in recollection. How can things be better for this man?

"Suppose, on the other hand, a man crushed beneath the heaviest load of mental and bodily pain that can befall a human being. Grant to him no hope of ultimate relief. Nor does he have neither present pleasure nor any expectation of any pleasure to come. Can one describe or imagine a more miserable condition?

"If then a life full of pain is the thing most to be avoided, it follows that to live in pain is the highest evil. This judgment implies that to live with pleasure is the ultimate good. In fact, the mind possesses nothing in itself upon which it can rest as final. Every fear, every sorrow can be traced back to pain. There is no other thing beside pain that is by its own nature able to disturb or torment.

[42] "Pleasure and pain moreover supply the motives of desire and of avoidance, and the springs of conduct generally. This being so, it clearly follows that actions are right and praiseworthy only when they are a means by which one may live with pleasure. But that which is not itself a means to anything else, but to which everything else is a means, is the highest or ultimate or final good. It is what the Greeks term *telos*, the end or goal of life. It must therefore be admitted that the highest good is to live in an agreeable manner.

"Those who place the highest good in virtue alone are captivated by the splendor of a name, and do not understand the true demands of nature. If they will consent to listen to Epicurus, they will be liberated from the greatest error. Your *Stoic* school goes on about the extraordinary beauty of the virtues. But if they did not produce pleasure, who would judge them either praiseworthy or desirable? We prize the art of medicine not for its interest as a science but for its conduciveness to good health. The art of navigation is commended for its practical and not its scientific value, because it conveys the rules for sailing a ship with success. The same is true for wisdom, which must be regarded as the art of living. If wisdom brought about nothing good, it would not be sought after. But as things stand, it is sought after because it is the skilled worker that procures and produces pleasure." [43] . . .

"Ignorance regarding good and evil is the one great disturbing factor in the life of men. Error about these often deprives us of our greatest pleasures and tortures us with the most distressing pains of mind. So it is that we need the aid of wisdom to rid us of our fears and desires, to root out all our false beliefs and thoughtlessness, and to serve as our infallible guide to the attainment of pleasure. Truly it is wisdom alone that can drive sorrow away from our souls and prevent us from trembling in fear. Go to school with her, and you may live in peace, quenching the glowing flames of desire.

"For the desires are insatiable. They ruin not only individual men but whole families. They often overthrow the republic all at once. [44] Hatred, disagreement, discord, sedition, and war are born from desires. Nor do they only flaunt themselves abroad or turn their blind onslaughts solely against others. Even when kept within the soul they quarrel and fall out among themselves. And this inevitably makes the whole of life bitter.

"So only the wise one who prunes away all vanity and error can possibly live untroubled by grief and fear, content within the bounds that nature has set.

[45] "Nothing could be more useful or more conducive to living well than Epicurus' teaching regarding the different kinds of desires. He said that one kind is both natural and necessary. Another is natural without being necessary. A third is neither natural nor necessary. The principle of classification is that the necessary desires are satisfied with little trouble or expense. The natural desires also require little, since nature's own riches, which are enough to make her content, are both easily procured and limited in amount. But for the imaginary, empty desires, it is impossible to discover either a measure or an end to them.

[46] "If then we observe that error and ignorance reduce the whole of life to confusion, while wisdom alone is able to protect us from the onslaughts of passion and the menaces of fear, teaching us to bear even the affronts of fortune with moderation, and showing us all the paths that lead to calmness and peace, why should we hesitate to avow that wisdom is to be desired for the sake of the pleasures it brings and folly to be avoided because of its troublesome consequences?

[47] "The same principle will lead us to declare that moderation also is not desirable for its own sake but because it bestows peace

of mind, and it calms the heart with a peaceful sense of harmony. For it is moderation that warns us to be guided by reason in what we seek and what we avoid. Nor is it enough to judge what it is right to do or to leave undone—we also need to abide by our judgment. Most men, however, are unable to stand firm. Their resolution weakens and succumbs as soon as the fair form of pleasure meets their gaze, and they surrender themselves prisoners to their passions, failing to foresee the inevitable result. So it is that for the sake of a pleasure at once small and unnecessary, and one which they might have procured by other means or even denied themselves altogether without pain, they experience a serious disease, or loss of fortune, or disgrace, and often they are penalized by the law within the courts of justice.

[48] "On the other hand, those who are resolved to enjoy their pleasures so as to avoid all painful consequences from them, and who retain their faculty of judgment and avoid being seduced by pleasure into courses that they perceive to be wrong, attain the very highest pleasure by forgoing pleasure. Similarly, they also often voluntarily endure pain in order to avoid experiencing greater pain by not doing so. This clearly proves that immoderation is not undesirable for its own sake, while moderation is desirable not because it shuns pleasures, but because it procures greater pleasures.

[49] "The same account also holds for courage. The performance of labors, the bearing of pains, are not in themselves attractive, nor are endurance, industry, watchfulness, nor yet that much lauded virtue, diligence, nor even courage. But we aim at these virtues in order to live without trouble or anxiety within our soul and body, and without fear, and so far as possible to be free from distress. The fear of death disturbs the calm and even tenor of life. And to bow the head to pain and bear it abjectly and feebly is a wretched thing. Such weakness has caused many men to betray their parents or their friends, and some their fatherland, and very many utterly to ruin themselves. So, on the other hand, a strong and lofty soul is entirely free from anxiety and torment. It makes light of death, for the dead are only as they were before they were born. It is schooled to encounter pain by recollecting that pains of great severity are terminated by

death, and that slight ones decrease now and then, while those of medium intensity are within our own control—that is, we can bear them if they are endurable, or, if they are not, we may serenely quit life's theatre when the play has ceased to please us. These considerations prove that timidity and cowardice are not blamed, nor courage and endurance praised, on their own account. The former are rejected because they produce pain, and the latter are preferred because they produce pleasure.

[50] "It remains to speak of justice—to complete the list of the virtues. But this virtue can practically be treated in the same way as the others. I have shown that wisdom, moderation, and courage are so intricately linked with pleasure that they cannot possibly be separated or divided from it. The same must be judged to be the case with justice. Not only does justice never cause anyone harm, but, on the contrary, it always adds some strength or benefit, partly because of its essentially calming influence on the soul, partly because of the hope that it guarantees a never-failing supply of the things that nature—uncorrupted, unspoiled—really wants.

"And just as thoughtlessness, passion, and cowardice always torment the soul, as well as disturb and cause storms in the soul, so wickedness, when seated in the mind, causes disturbance by the mere fact of its presence. And once one commits an act of wickedness, however secret the act, one may never feel sure that it will always remain a secret. What usually follows upon a wicked act are, first, suspicion; next, gossip and rumor; then, the accuser comes and the judge. Many wrongdoers have even informed against themselves, as happened in your consulship. [51] And even if any think themselves well guarded and fortified against detection by their fellow-men, they still dread the gods and believe that the anxiety devouring their souls by night and by day is sent by the immortal gods to punish them.

"But how can wickedness lessen the troubles of life, when it increases them thanks to conscience and the penalties of the law and the animosity of one's fellow citizens? Even so, some men indulge without limit their avarice, ambition and love of power, passions, gluttony, and those other desires, which ill-gotten gain can never reduce but rather must inflame all the more—so that it appears that these desires must be restrained more than unlearned.

[52] "Men of sound natures, therefore, are summoned by the voice of true reason to justice, fairness, and honesty. For the man of low status or no power, wrongful behavior is not profitable since it is difficult for such a man to succeed in his designs or to keep up his success when once achieved. On the other hand, for the rich and clever, generous conduct seems more appropriate, and liberality wins them affection and good will, the surest means to a life of peace and quiet. This is so particularly because there really is no motive for making any mistakes or committing any transgressions, [53] since the desires that originate with nature are easily satisfied without wronging anyone, while those that are empty or imaginary should be resisted given that they desire nothing at all that is truly desirable. Not only that, but there is more loss inherent in wrongdoing itself than there is profit in the gains that wrongdoing brings. So, we cannot correctly say that injustice is desirable in itself. It is only so thanks to the all the enjoyment it can produce. . . .

"Therefore, we hold that wickedness should be avoided not only because of the inconveniences that result from wickedness but even far more because when it whirls and whirls in the soul, it never gives the soul a chance to rest or be quiet.

[54] "If then even the glory of the virtues, on which all the other philosophers particularly love to speak, has no significance unless virtue is directed to pleasure—since in comparison with virtue, pleasure is the only thing that is satisfying, naturally calling us to itself—it cannot be doubted that pleasure is the highest and final of all the goods, and that to live happily is nothing other than to live with pleasure.

[55] "The view thus firmly established has corollaries that I will briefly explain. One, in themselves, the ends of good things and bad things, that is, pleasure and pain, are not open to mistake. Where people go wrong is in not knowing what things produce pleasure and pain.

"Two, again, we aver that pleasures and pains of the soul arise from the pleasures and pains of the body (and therefore I allow your contention that any Epicureans who think otherwise fail in their cause; and I am aware that many do, though not those who can speak with authority). Even though we experience mental pleasure that is delightful and mental pain that is annoying, still, both arise from the body and return to the body.

"Three, nevertheless, we maintain that the aforementioned does not prevent pleasures and pains of the soul from being much greater than those of the body. For the body can feel only what is present to it at the moment, whereas the soul can also sense the past and the future. Granting that pain of the body is equally painful, yet our sensation of pain can be enormously increased by the belief that some evil of unlimited magnitude and duration threatens to befall us hereafter. And the same consideration may be transferred to pleasure: a pleasure is greater if not accompanied by any fear of evil. [56] This is clearly the case, then: that great pleasure or distress of soul contributes more to a happy or miserable life than does pleasure and pain of the body that is equal.

"Four, we do not agree that when pleasure is withdrawn, affliction at once follows, unless the pleasure happens to have been replaced by a pain. By contrast, one is glad to lose a pain even though no active sensation of pleasure follows—so one can understand how the absence of pain is pleasure.

[57] "But—five—just as we are elated by the expectation of good things, so are we delighted by their recollection. Fools are tormented by the memory of former evils, while wise men have the delight of renewing in grateful remembrance past goods. We have the power both to hide our misfortunes in an almost perpetual forgetfulness and to summon up pleasant and agreeable memories of our successes. But when we fix our mental gaze closely on the events of the past, then sorrow or gladness follow depending on if these were evil or good.

"I proclaim that here is a very bright road to living happily—an open way, simple and direct. For clearly a human can have no greater good than complete freedom from pain and distress coupled with the enjoyment of the greatest pleasures of the body and soul.

"See then how the theory embraces every possible enhancement of life, every aid to the attainment of that highest good, which is our object. Epicurus, the man whom you denounce as a voluptuary, cries aloud that no one can live pleasantly without living wisely, honorably, and justly—and that no one can live wisely, honorably, and justly without living pleasantly. [58] For truly, it is impossible for a city torn by civil discord to be happy and prosper. The same is true for a house where there is disagreement among the masters. Even less, then, is it possible for a soul that is divided against itself and filled with inward discord to taste any bit of pure and unimpeded pleasure. No—the one who always has inconsistent resolutions and contradictory inclinations cannot experience quiet or tranquility.

[59] "If the enjoyment of life is hindered by the more serious bodily illnesses, how much more must it be hindered by the illnesses of the soul. But extravagant and imaginary desires—for riches, fame, power, and also for licentious pleasures—are nothing but illnesses of the soul. There are grief, distress, and sorrow, which devour the soul and consume a human being with anxiety if one does not understand that there is no pain in the soul, now or in the future, that is not connected with bodily pain. Every fool is oppressed by one of these illnesses; therefore, there is no fool who is not miserable. [60] There is also death, the stone of Tantalus, that is forever hanging over our heads. And there is superstition, which poisons and destroys all peace. Moreover, fools do not recall past goods, nor do they enjoy present goods; rather, they merely await future goods. And since these goods are necessarily uncertain, they are consumed with the greatest agony and fear. And the climax of their torment is when they perceive too late that all their dreams of wealth or power, influence or fame, have come to nothing. For truly pleasures do not result from these—the pleasures that set them on fire to take on many and great toils.

[61] "Or look again at others who are petty, narrow-minded men, or confirmed pessimists, or spiteful, envious, ill-tempered creatures, unsociable, abusive, and brutal, or others given over to the shallowness of sensual love, impudent or reckless, wanton, headstrong and yet irresolute, always changing their minds. Because of this, their

lives have no break from distress. So it is that no fool is happy. Nor is there any wise man who is not happy. This is a truth that we establish far more conclusively than do the Stoics. . . .

[62] "At the same time this Stoic doctrine can be stated in an unobjectionable form—one, in fact, that we Epicureans approve. For Epicurus presents his wise man as always happy in this way: his desires are kept within bounds; he disregards death; he has a true understanding of the immortal gods; he does not hesitate, if it is better, to depart from life. Prepared in this manner, he enjoys perpetual pleasure since there is no moment when the pleasures he experiences do not outweigh the pains. He remembers the past with gratitude and grasps the present, giving mind to its delight, and does not rely on the future. He expects to enjoy these delights in the present. Moreover, the vices I mentioned a few moments ago are entirely absent. When he compares his life with that of foolish men, he experiences great pleasure. But if the wise man meets up with pains, they are never so severe that the anguish is more than the joy.

[63] "Again, Epicurus says well that 'fortune barely hinders the wise man. The great concerns of life, the things that matter, are directed by his own deliberation and reason.' And this, that 'no greater pleasure could be obtained from a life of infinite duration than is actually obtained by this existence that we know to be finite.'

"He held that logic is not important as a guide to conduct or as an aid to thought. Natural philosophy he judged all-important. This science explains to us the meaning of terms, the nature of predication, and the law of consistency and contradiction. Secondly, a thorough knowledge of the facts of nature relieves us of the burden of superstition, frees us from the fear of death, and shields us against the disturbing effects of ignorance, from which horrible and dreadful things often manifest. Lastly, to learn what nature's real requirements are improves the moral character also. Besides, it is only by firmly grasping a well-established scientific system, observing the rule or canon that has fallen, as it were, from heaven so that all men may know it—it is only by making that canon the test of all our judgments that we can hope always to stand fast in our belief, unshaken by the eloquence of any man.

[64] "On the other hand, without a full understanding of natural things, it is impossible to maintain the criterion of sense perceptions. Further, every mental presentation has its origin in sensation. So it is that no certain knowledge will be possible unless all sensations are true—just as the theory of Epicurus teaches they are. Those who deny the validity of sensation and say that nothing can be perceived are not even able to expound their own argument since they have excluded the evidence of the senses. Moreover, by abolishing knowledge and science, they abolish all possibility of rational life and action. Hence, natural philosophy supplies courage to face the dread of death, and consistency to resist the fear of religious phenomena, and a calming of the soul to take away all ignorance regarding the mysteries and every secret thing, and moderation and self-control by explaining the nature of the desires and their different kinds. And, as I showed just now, the canon or criterion of knowledge, which Epicurus also established, delivers a way to distinguish between a true thing and a false thing.

[65] "There remains a topic that is quite necessary for this discussion—that of friendship. . . . About it, Epicurus says this: that of all the means of living happily that wisdom has devised, none is greater, none is more productive, none is more delightful than friendship. Nor did he only establish this in truth by his speaking alone but much more by his life—in what he did and how he behaved. . . . In a single, small house, Epicurus hosted a large group of friends united by the closest sympathy and affection. And this still goes on in the Epicurean school. . . .

[66] ". . . Friendship can no more be separated from pleasure than can the virtues, which we have discussed already. A solitary, friendless life is necessarily plagued by secret dangers and plenty of fear. Therefore, reason itself advises the acquisition of friends. Having them makes one strong and offers the hope of being able to experience pleasure.

[67] "And just as hatred, jealousy, and contempt are hindrances to pleasure, so friendship is the most trustworthy protector—and producer—of pleasure. This is so both for our friends and ourselves. Not only is it enjoyable in the present but it inspires us with

hope for the near and distant future. So, it is not possible to possess a stable and ongoing delight in life without friendship.

"Moreover, it is not possible to maintain friendship itself unless we value our friends as much as we value ourselves. Therefore, this unselfishness itself is brought about in friendship—this, while friendship is also closely linked with pleasure. For we rejoice in our friends' joy as much as in our own, and we are equally pained by their anxieties. [68] Therefore, the wise man will feel exactly the same toward his friend as he does toward himself, and he will exert himself as much for his friend's pleasure as he would for his own. . . .

[71] "If then the teachings I have related are noble and clear; if everything I have said is drawn from the well of nature; if my whole discourse is confirmed by the reliability of the senses; if, prompted by the voice of nature, unspoiled and untouched baby children and speechless animals nearly find a voice to proclaim that there is nothing more fortunate than pleasure and nothing more troublesome than pain;—if so, then should we not feel the greatest gratitude for the man who caught this utterance of nature's voice and grasped its significance so firmly and so fully that he has led all good and healthy men into the way of a life of calmness and tranquility, quiet and happiness?"

NOTES

[1] "Pleasure" here is *voluptas*. In Book 2 of Cicero's *On the Ends of Good Things and Bad Things*, M. Cato states, "I mean the same by 'pleasure' as Epicurus does by *hēdonē*. One often has some trouble discovering a Latin word that is the precise equivalent of a Greek word. In this case, however, no search was necessary. No instance can be found of a Latin word that more exactly conveys the same meaning as the corresponding Greek word than does the word *voluptas*. Every person in the world who knows Latin attaches to this word two ideas— that of gladness of mind, and that of a delightful excitation of agreeable feeling in the body" (2.13).

[2] The translation that follows is a modified version of H. Rackham's translation of *De Finibus Bonorum et Malorum* (1914)—typically given as *On the Ends of Good and Evil*.

PART 6

POINTS OF WISDOM & WAYS OF PRACTICE
FROM EPICURUS

- A Plan of Life
Following the Philosophy of Epicurus

- Points of Wisdom from Epicurus

- Ways of Practice Following Epicurus

A Plan of Life
Following the Philosophy of Epicurus

A S WITH ANY other plan, a plan of life is made to accomplish certain goals or possibly just one significant goal. In the case of this plan of life, the goal is happiness in terms of tranquility. It consists of the most significant goals and practices inspired by Epicurus and Epicureanism.

1. **Act. Do.** Take care of and do those things which produce happiness. Be active not passive. Realize that doing is everything. Happiness is not something that happens to us but something we choose and do. Choose happiness. Do happiness.

2. **Practice day and night.** The good life is a full-time practice. Why would anyone wish to take time off from happiness?

3. **Exercise by yourself and with others who are like-minded.** Resolve to practice when alone. Find strength in others who are similarly committed to the good life. Beware of those who are not: "Disregard those who are ignorant of what makes tranquility possible or what prevents it."

4. **Desire well; practice desire reduction.** For the greatest happiness, limit yourself to the satisfaction of natural and necessary desires. Avoid satisfying those desires that are unnatural and unnecessary, those that originate in groundless notions. Mind the measure of pleasure. "The standard measure for the greatest amount of pleasure is the removal of every pain. Whenever pleasure is present, as long as it lasts, there is neither pain nor distress nor both together."

5. **Endure pain.** When necessary, put up with pain in order to avoid further or other pain and to experience greater pleasure, peace, and happiness.

6. **Strive for self-sufficiency.** Be satisfied with little. Pursue simple pleasures. Get used to basic and inexpensive foods and other things. Drink water. "A barley cake and water offer the highest possible pleasure when they are given to a hungry man." Everything natural and beneficial is easy to get. Seek quality over quantity.

7. **Practice friendship.** Trust. Be giving and kind. Be grateful. Recall the good times and the beneficial conversations you have had with friends. Care for and advise one another.

8. **Cultivate the virtues.** Seek excellence. "The virtues have become one with living pleasantly, . . . [which] is inseparable from the virtues." Live wisely. Be noble and just, moderate and courageous.

9. **Seek knowledge and wisdom.** Do philosophy in order to have a healthy soul and be happy. Keep in mind that all theoretical work is best oriented to practice—for the purpose of tranquility. Realize there is truly nothing to fear or worry about.

10. **Know well.** Practice careful sensation and deliberate judgment. Understand the criteria of truth (sensations, preconceptions, and feelings). Always follow the facts. Realize that some things are impossible to know (so do not force the matter; be content with what you are actually able to know). Many points must simply "await confirmation"—that is, await further information. There are levels of clarity, from single to multiple explanations. Do not accept arbitrary laws or empty assumptions.

11. **Utilize epitomes.** Begin with summaries and work toward the details of your philosophical system. The basic system should answer what and how we can know; what is real; and how we can be at peace (be happy). Simplicity sets the stage for complexity—the general for the specific.

12. **Memorize, review, recall.** Learn an elementary outline by heart. Return to it often. Keep in mind the principal points and use them as aids to practice and further understanding.

POINTS OF WISDOM
FROM EPICURUS

The following points of wisdom come from Epicurus' writings, either found in Diogenes Laertius' Lives *or in the* Vatican Sayings. *Each point begins in italics with a word indicating the point's topic or a brief summary. For more points of wisdom organized by topic, read The Classics Cave's* The Wisdom & Way of Epicurus & Epicureanism.

The time for philosophy is now Let no one put off studying philosophy when he is young, nor become weary of it when he is old, for no age is too early or too late for the health of the soul. To suggest that the time for studying philosophy has not yet come or that it is long gone is like saying that it is too early or too late for happiness.

Do philosophy We must not merely pretend to practice philosophy; rather, we must actually do it. For we do not merely need the appearance of health, but true health.

Ponder the goal of life The better man is the one who has considered the natural goal of life. . . . The goal of a blessedly happy life is to secure bodily health and mental tranquility.

Rise to happiness with a friend Friendship dances around the world of men calling out to all of us, "Rise up to happiness!"

Practice happiness We must practice those things that produce happiness since if happiness is present, we possess everything, and if it is not, we do everything to acquire it.

Seize the day We come into being only once and will not be born a second time. Rather, we necessarily will never exist again—forever. And though you have no power over tomorrow, you put off feeling joy today. Life is consumed by such indecision and procrastination! And so, each one of us is dying without engaging in life today.

Focus on what is absolutely necessary Our one need is to live undisturbed, without trouble. We have come to the point where our life has no need for non-rational and empty opinion.

Keep the goal in mind Everything we do is for the sake of being free from pain and from fear. The soul's storm scatters as soon as we achieve this condition. Then we have no need to go around looking for anything that is lacking or seeking something else by which the good of the soul and the good of the body will be fulfilled.

Do not seek what cannot procure tranquility Soul-disturbance is not resolved, nor is true joy produced, by the possession of the greatest wealth, nor by the honor and admiration of the many, nor by any other thing that is the result of indefinite factors.

Keep in mind: we all die Some men spend their whole lives procuring for themselves those things necessary to life without grasping that each of us was poured a mortal mixture to drink at our birth.

Know the basic kinds of desire Of the desires, some are natural, and some are groundless. Of the natural desires, some are necessary, and some are merely natural. And of the necessary desires, some are necessary for happiness, some for freeing the body from disturbance, and some for living itself.

Be aware of the nature of unnecessary desire Unnecessary desires are those that lead to no pain if they remain unsatisfied. They involve an appetite that is easily relieved whenever its satisfaction is hard to procure or when it seems likely to cause harm.

Strive to obey nature when satisfying your desires We must obey nature rather than doing violence to her. We will obey nature by satisfying the necessary desires and the natural desires, too, as long as they do no harm, but sharply rejecting the harmful desires.

Realize the difference between natural and groundless things Everything natural is easy to get, but whatever is groundless is hard.

Pleasure is the goal of life For proof that pleasure is the goal of life, Epicurus points to the fact that living things, as soon as they are born, are quite satisfied with pleasure, whereas they are naturally upset with pain—and this without rational reflection.

Know the parameters of the need for pleasure We have the need for pleasure only when we feel pain due to the absence of pleasure. When we feel no pain, however, there is no need for pleasure. For this reason, we say that pleasure is the beginning point and goal of living happily. We recognize that pleasure is our first good, present at birth, and that it is the beginning point of every choice and avoidance. We resort to pleasure when we use feeling as the measure for judging every good.

Know the measure of pleasure The standard measure for the greatest amount of pleasure is the removal of every pain. Whenever pleasure is present, as long as it lasts, there is neither pain nor distress nor both together.

Understand how pleasure may increase (or not) Pleasure in the flesh will not increase after need-based pain is removed. After that, pleasure may only be varied.

When to choose pleasure and when to allow pain—know the advantages and disadvantages Even though pleasure is our first and inborn good, we nevertheless do not choose every pleasure. Rather, we often-times forgo many pleasures when a greater annoyance will follow from choosing them. And oftentimes we acknowledge that many pains are better than many pleasures when an even greater pleasure follows from patiently enduring these pains for a long period of time. And so, even though every pleasure is naturally good and fitting, not every pleasure is to be chosen. In the same way, even though every pain is bad, not every pain is always to be avoided.

To be sure, we may aptly judge every case by measuring one feeling in comparison with the other and taking a look at the advantages and disadvantages of both sides. Sometimes we treat a good thing as though it is bad. On the other hand, sometimes we treat a bad thing as though it is good.

(True) pleasure as the absence of pain and trouble—and the need for reason When we say that pleasure is the beginning point and goal of life, we do not mean the pleasures of decadent men or the pleasures of sensuality, as some ignorant persons believe, or those who do not agree with us, or those who have willfully misrepresented our position. Rather, by pleasure we mean the absence of pain in the body and of trouble in the soul. A pleasant life is not produced by stringing together one drinking party after another, or by having sex with young boys or women, or by enjoying fish and other delicacies set on a luxurious table. Instead, it is produced by sober reasoning that examines what is responsible for every choice and avoidance, and expels those beliefs by which the greatest confusion lays hold of the soul.

Sex Epicureans say that sexual intercourse never benefited anyone. One must be content if it has not caused harm.

Soul versus body pleasures Epicurus believes that pleasures of the soul are greater than those of the body.

Realize the good of self-sufficiency We regard self-sufficiency as a great good not so that we may enjoy just a little in every case, but so that when things are scarce, we may nevertheless be satisfied with little, genuinely persuaded that the ones who derive the greatest pleasure from luxury are the ones who need it the least, and that everything natural is easy to get, but whatever is groundless is hard.

Simple food (versus gourmet or rich food) Simple food gives just as much pleasure as rich food does as soon as the hunger pains are gone. A barley cake and water offer the highest possible pleasure when they are given to a hungry man. Getting used to simple and inexpensive food, therefore, aids the health of a man and enables him to perform the necessary requirements of life with resolution. Not only that, but such a habit better disposes us for when we encounter extravagant fare now and again, and makes us fearless in the face of fortune.

The benefit of (just) enough Epicurus declares that if he has enough bread, then he is not inferior to the gods regarding happiness.

Enjoy what is present You must not ruin what is present by a longing for what is absent; rather, keep in mind that these things were what you previously desired.

Be satisfied with enough Nothing is enough for someone for whom enough is very little.

Practical wisdom and other virtues Practical wisdom is the greatest good. For this reason, we value practical wisdom even more than philosophy. Every other virtue is produced from practical wisdom, teaching us that we cannot live pleasantly without living wisely, nobly, and justly—just as we cannot live wisely, nobly, and justly without living pleasantly. The virtues have become one with living pleasantly. Living pleasantly is inseparable from the virtues.

Let reason manage the things of life Luck rarely interferes with the wise man. Rather, it is reason that has managed, does manage, and will manage the greatest and most essential things throughout the course of a wise man's life.

The rational life is one pursuing nature's goal If at any moment you do not direct each of your actions to the goal of life indicated by nature, but, instead, you turn aside to some other goal in the act of pursuing some object or avoiding it, your activity will not be consistent with the conclusions drawn from reason.

Pursue friendship for the sake of happiness Of all the means that are procured by wisdom to ensure blessed happiness throughout the whole of life, by far the most important is the acquisition of friend-ship.

Friendship and happiness Friendship dances around the world of men calling out to all of us, "Rise up to happiness!"

Act to avoid fear Do nothing in your life that will cause you fear if discovered by your neighbor.

Reputation The approval of others is necessarily their own business. As for us, we must get on with our own healing.

Peace leads to peace The man who is free from disturbance within himself is no trouble to another man.

The causes of harm and the solution (reason) Harm arises among men through hatred, envy, and contempt. The wise man skirts these by means of reason.

Death means nothing to us Death—that evil which most causes us to shudder—means nothing to us since when we exist, death is not present, and when death is present, we do not exist. In fact, death means nothing either to the living or to those who have finished living since it does not exist for the former, and the latter no longer exist.

The benefit of understanding what death is A right understanding of the fact that death means nothing to us makes the mortal nature of life beneficial to us—not by adding to life an unlimited amount of time, but by taking away the yearning for immortality. For there is no terror at all in living for the one who has thoroughly grasped that there is no terror at all in not living. Foolish, therefore, is the man who says that he fears death because it pains him to think about its eventual coming rather than actually paining him when it comes. Whatever causes no trouble when it is present causes only a groundless pain in its mere anticipation.

Ways of Practice
Following Epicurus

The following ways of practice, inspired by Epicurus and his writings, are offered with the goal of practice in mind, the application of ancient wisdom to our contemporary ways and lives. We hope they will serve, in some small measure, as a source of inspiration and motivation. Use them to contemplate your life—where you are now, where you are going, and how you can better get there. For these exercises and practices and other similar ones, pick up The Classics Cave's Epicurus & Epicureanism Workbook & Journal. *One last note. You will likely find that the space given for responses is not enough. If so, jot your thoughts and practices down in a separate place.*

Practice 1: Soul Storms—Living with Soul-Disturbance

"Everything we do is for the sake of being free from pain and from fear. The soul's storm scatters as soon as we achieve this condition. Then we have no need to go around looking for anything that is lacking or seeking something else by which the good of the soul and the good of the body will be fulfilled." —Epicurus

"Soul-disturbance is not resolved, nor is true joy produced, by the possession of the greatest wealth, nor by the honor and admiration of the many, nor by any other thing that is the result of indefinite factors." —Epicurus

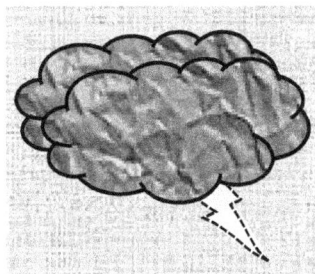

The soul's storm Most of us experience any number of obstacles to happiness. Gathered in all their ferocity and force, Epicurus calls these obstacles "the soul's storm," a combination of thundering pain, downpouring fear, pounding waves of disturbance, and gusting inner trouble. The question is, What do we do when the weather of the soul shifts with black clouds appearing and rolling thunder sounding over the horizon? As always, the best place to begin is with some reflection.

SOUL METEOROLOGY • Knowing, Predicting & Living with Soul Storms

Meteorologists know the various factors that make for storms and what causes them. Knowing these, they learn how to predict their appearance and give advice regarding how to live with them.

Q • What internal and external factors build to produce my "soul storms"? Asked another way, what causes me to feel any sort of soul-disturbance—anxiety, fear, anger, irritation, depression, sadness?

_____

_____

_____

_____

_____

_____

_____

(Circle one)

I   know / do not know   the signs that indicate the approach of
my soul storms.

Q • If I circled know, what are the signs? If I circled do not know, what can I do to learn the signs? How can I better live with my soul storms?

PRACTICE 2: TRANQUILITY — CULTIVATING INNER PEACE & HEALING

"The goal of a blessedly happy life is to secure bodily health and mental tranquility." — Epicurus

"We must disregard those who are ignorant of what makes tranquility possible." — Epicurus

"Our one need is to live undisturbed, without trouble. We have come to the point in life where our life has no need for non-rational and empty opinion." — Epicurus

"As for us, we must get on with our own healing." — Epicurus

TRANQUILITY · For Epicurus, the opposite of a soul storm is a kind of stillness. When the storm scatters, the waters are still and the sun shines. This soul condition, Epicurus contends, is the goal of a happy life. It is to be at peace in mind and body — tranquil. It is to be healed in body and soul.

Q · What is it like when I feel tranquil? What sort of thoughts do I have when I feel at peace? What do I feel? What sort of things am I doing when tranquil? Am I typically alone or with others? If with others, who?

TRANQUILITY LIST · Identify a daily, a weekly, and a monthly thing I can do to scatter the soul's storm and cultivate inner peace and healing:

PRACTICE 3: *CARPE DIEM*—SEIZING THE DAY

"We come into being only once and will not be born a second time. Rather, we necessarily will never exist again—forever. And though you have no power over tomorrow, you put off feeling joy today. Life is consumed by such indecision and procrastination! And so, each one of us is dying without engaging in life today." —Epicurus

"Some men spend their whole lives procuring for themselves those things necessary for life without grasping that each of us was poured a mortal mixture to drink at our birth." —Epicurus

Contemplation 1 • Take a few moments to contemplate what it means to exist—*to be.*

Say to yourself, slowly— *I AM.   I AM.   I AM.*

Say to yourself, slowly— *I EXIST.   I EXIST.   I EXIST.*

What feelings appear in your innermost self when you say, "I am" and "I exist"? What thoughts come to mind? What does such a contemplation make you want to do?

Contemplation 2 • Take a few moments to consider the fact that you have no power over tomorrow, whether it will come for you or not. Consequently, this present moment is the only one you can be sure of.

What feelings arise in you? What thoughts bubble up? What does such a reflection urge you to do?

Q · Am I living for today? Or more for tomorrow?

_____

_____

_____

_____

_____

Q · How can I engage in life today? How can I seize the day (*carpe diem*)? What can I regularly do?—minute by minute, hour by hour, day by day, week by week?

_____

_____

_____

_____

_____

Q · How can I feel joy today? What can I regularly do?—minute by minute, hour by hour, day by day, week by week?

_____

_____

_____

Intently building a sandcastle.

OTHER MATTERS OF INTEREST
RELATED TO EPICURUS & EPICUREANISM

THE CAST OF SIGNIFICANT EPICUREANS
A QUICK REFERENCE & CHRONOLOGY

THE FOUNDING—late fourth into the third century BC

EPICURUS: the son of Neocles and Chaerestrate; born in Samos in 341 BC. Influenced by earlier Greek philosophy, Epicurus developed and promoted his philosophy (one of four great ancient Greek schools) from "the Garden" in Athens, after having lived and taught philosophy in Mytilene (on the island of Lesbos) and Lampsacus (along the Hellespont, now the Dardanelles). Epicurus taught that if we could limit ourselves to what can actually be known about reality, then we will obtain happiness, the goal of life. There is no need to fear the gods or death. We need only to satisfy natural and necessary desires and to pay attention to the measure of pleasure (and pain) in order to live in a state of tranquility. Epicurus taught and lived a simple, frugal life (contrary to the modern meaning of epicureanism). He strongly believed in the value of friendship. We possess three major letters of Epicurus (to Herodotus, to Pythocles, and to Menoeceus) and several collections of his principal teachings and sayings. Epicurus died c. 270 BC.

THE EARLY EPICUREANS—late fourth into the third century BC

COLOTES OF LAMPSACUS (on the Hellespont) (c. 325-260 BC): a favorite of Epicurus. Plutarch relates that when Colotes heard Epicurus teach about the nature of things, he fell on his knees and begged him to instruct him. He also suggests that he was clever but dogmatic. Colotes famously wrote a work that explained how impossible it was to live according to the teachings of the other non-Epicurean philosophers. Like Epicurus, Colotes insisted that theory must (be able to) result in practice.

HERMARCHUS OF MYTILENE (on the island of Lesbos): the son of Agemortus; one of Epicurus' most faithful students and friends, Hermarchus wrote several polemical books against the philosophies of Plato and Aristotle, among others. He denied the existence of the atomist Leucippus. When Epicurus died, he left Hermarchus in charge of the Epicurean school. He also gave him his Garden and books.

HERODOTUS: one of Epicurus' students. Epicurus wrote a letter to him, the *Letter to Herodotus*, in which he offers an epitome of his philosophy of nature.

IDOMENEUS OF LAMPSACUS (on the Hellespont) (c. 325-c. 270 BC): one of Epicurus' students and close friends. He wrote several philosophical and historical works. He married Batis, the sister of Metrodorus. Epicurus' last letter was addressed to Idomeneus. In it, Epicurus joyfully recalls all their discussions.

MENOECEUS: one of Epicurus' students. Epicurus wrote a letter to him, the *Letter to Menoeceus*, in which he offers counsel on how to do philosophy and practice happiness.

METRODORUS OF LAMPSACUS (on the Hellespont) (c. 331-278 BC): the son of Athenaeus (or of Timocrates) and of Sande; Epicurus' closest follower and friend. He gave his sister Batis to Idomeneus to marry, while he took Leontion, the Athenian prostitute, as his mistress. He wrote many books on a variety of subjects—the sensations, the journey to wisdom, and nobility. The Epicurean school met on the twentieth of every month to commemorate Epicurus and Metrodorus. Epicurus left provisions for Metrodorus' son (Epicurus) and daughter in his will. Brave in the face of death, Metrodorus died seven or eight years before Epicurus.

MYS (Mouse): Epicurus' slave. Mys joined his master in the study of philosophy. Along with Nicias, Lycon, and Phaedrium, Mys was emancipated upon Epicurus' death (according to his will).

NEOCLES, CHAEREDEMUS, AND ARISTOBULUS: Epicurus' three brothers, who joined him in studying philosophy. The Epicurean school joined together to commemorate them on a day in the month of Poseidon (part of December-January).

POLYAENUS OF LAMPSACUS (on the Hellespont): the son of Athenodorus; one of Epicurus students and close friends. Diogenes Laertius tells us that he was a gentle and friendly man. The Epicurean school joined together to commemorate him on a day in the month of Metageitnion (part of August-September).

PYTHOCLES: one of Epicurus' students. Epicurus wrote a letter to him, the *Letter to Pythocles*, in which he offers multiple explanations regarding phenomena in the sky as well as other natural phenomena.

THEMISTA AND LEONTEUS OF LAMPSACUS (on the Hellespont): married, they were both Epicureans. They called their son Epicurus. Diogenes Laertes reports that Epicurus dedicated his work, the *Neocles*, to Themista, and that he wrote letters to her.

THE SUCCESSORS OF EPICURUS IN THE EPICUREAN SCHOOL

Hermarchus succeeded Epicurus, followed by Polystratus, then Dionysus, Basilides, Apollodorus (the very prolific "tyrant of the Garden"; called Apollodorus the Epicurean by Diogenes Laertius, he wrote a *Life of Epicurus*), the two Ptolemies of Alexandria (one "black" [*melas*] and one "white" [*leukos*]), Zeno of Sidon (who was also prolific), Demetrius ("the Lacedaemonian"), Diogenes of Tarsus, Orion, and others.

EARLY ROMAN EPICUREANISM—first century BC

CALPURNIUS PISO CAESONINUS: the father-in-law of Julius Caesar. He was Philodemus of Gadara's patron and was likely the owner of the villa in Herculaneum, which held the library in which so many of Philodemus' works were found in the 1750s onwards. The library itself was buried when Mount Vesuvius erupted in 79 AD.

TITUS LUCRETIUS CARUS: Roman poet and author of the epic poem, *On the Nature of Things* (*De Rerum Natura*), in which he explains the logic and tenets of Epicureanism and lauds Epicurus as the liberator of humankind. Cicero admired the genius and craftmanship of his poetry. We know virtually nothing of Lucretius' life.

PHILODEMUS OF GADARA: from Gadara in Syria, Philodemus "studied Epicureanism in the Athenian Garden during Zeno of Sidon's" leadership of the school (first century BC). He ended up in southern Italy where he formed his own "Epicurean circle at Herculaneum," and was, according to Cicero, one of the most distinguished Epicurean philosophers of his time, influencing such Roman writers as Horace and Virgil. Philodemus was a voluminous writer, writing works on philosophical history, aesthetics, ethics, theology, epistemology, as well as a number of epigrams.

LUCIUS MANLIUS TORQUATUS: Roman statesman, whom Cicero presents as the spokesman for Epicureanism in his work, *On the Ends of Good Things and Bad Things (De Finibus Bonorum et Malorum).*

LATER EPICUREANS

DIOGENES OF OENOANDA (Oinoanda): a wealthy man who lived during the second century AD in the Roman province of Lycia in what is now south-western Turkey. He left an inscription on a long wall setting out the Epicurean path to understanding and happiness.

POMPEIA PLOTINA: wife of the Roman emperor Trajan (late first and early second century AD). An Epicurean, she actively supported the Epicurean school in Athens.

Greece and Asia Minor (Map 1)

Born on the island of Samos, Epicurus lived in Mytilene (Lesbos) and Lampsacus before settling in Athens, where he founded the Garden.

Note: some modern place names are given for purposes of orientation.

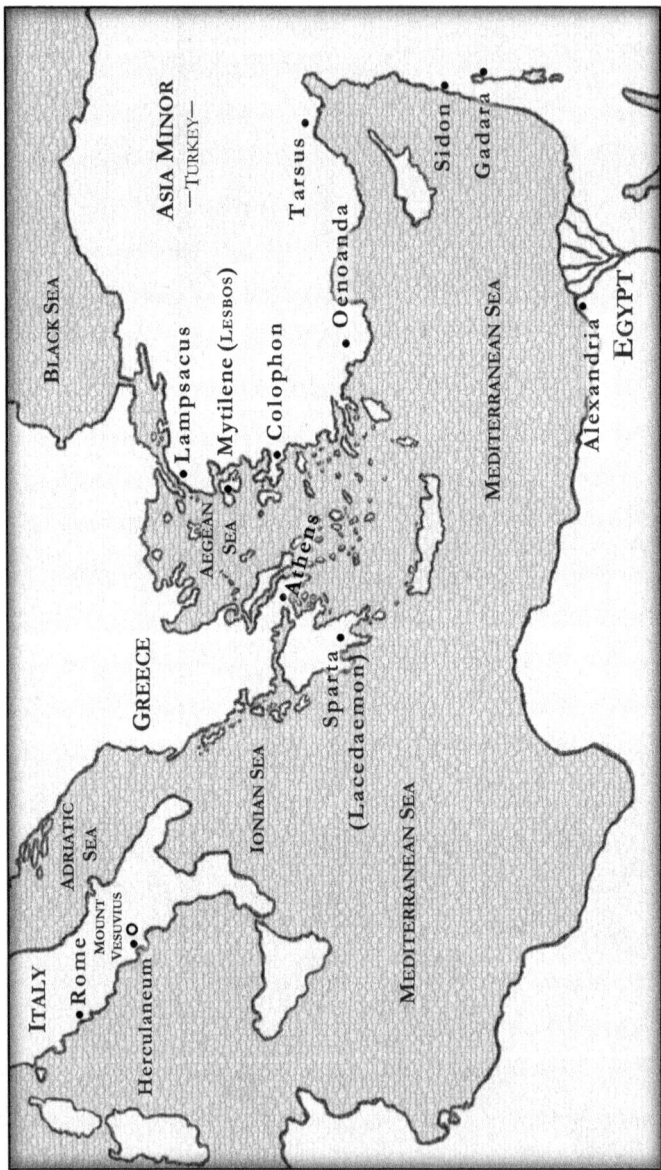

The Mediterranean World (Map 2)

Epicureans came from all over the ancient Mediterranean world, including each of the above cities.

Note: some modern place names are given for purposes of orientation.

General Summary
of the Letters of Epicurus

The Letter to Herodotus

AFTER GREETING HERODOTUS, Epicurus explains the purpose of the letter, which is to provide a general survey or epitome of his conclusions regarding the nature of reality. This will help Herodotus and "all who take up natural science" to "obtain a valid understanding of the facts," which will in turn aid them in further discovering the nature of things.

Regarding a general method, Epicurus reminds Herodotus to rely on clear terms and the criteria of sensation and feelings when investigating and drawing conclusions about things.

The first two major points are that "nothing comes into being out of what is non-existent" and that nothing completely falls into non-existence. Rather, considered as a whole, the sum of things is infinite and everlasting. Epicurus gives arguments for each of these points.

Everlasting and infinite, the cosmos has two basic elements, bodies and void. Bodies are either composite or non-composite. The latter non-composite bodies are the elements out of which the composite bodies are made. These non-composite bodies are "atoms"—indivisible, solid, indestructible. The whole of reality is infinite in terms of the number of atoms and the extent of the void.

Atoms have an indefinite number of shapes. Atomic shape accounts for the great variety of everything that has come to be. Atoms continually move, rebounding off one another or oscillating when entangled with or enclosed by a mass of other atoms.

The void allows for movement. Atoms have always moved in the void. There was no beginning nor will there ever be an end. Given the infinite number of atoms and the infinite size of the void, it follows that there is an infinite number of worlds.

Epicurus next explores the nature of seeing, hearing, and smelling, three ways by which we sense reality. Seeing happens by means of impression. Sold bodies or objects emanate outlines or films of themselves that rapidly move "as quick as thought" in multiple directions. When such an outline or image strikes the senses, it communicates the appearance (color, form, etc.) of the solid body or object. Consequently, there is direct contact with the senses, whether with the sense organ itself (e.g., the eyes) or the mind. The contact is like a mirror's reception of an image. Epicurus reminds Herodotus how important it is to stick with clear and distinct perceptions before moving on to discuss hearing and smelling.

He then expounds the qualities and motion of atoms. The basic qualities of all atoms are shape, weight, and size. Atoms do not have parts; they are indivisible or uncuttable (*atomos*). All atoms move at the same speed through the void. This speed is equal to the speed of thought.

Epicurus moves on to explore the corporeal or bodily nature of the soul and the significant role it has in sensation. When the soul departs, the rest of the human organism no longer has sensation. Neither does the soul (i.e., its now-scattered or uncontained atoms) have sensation when it is alone since the rest of the human organism "provides the indispensable condition" for the soul's powers of sensation.

Next, he describes what we sense in terms of properties and accidents, adding on a short reflection on how we should think and speak about time.

Moving on, he addresses the formation and breaking apart of multiple worlds from the infinite, the rise of plants and animals, and the evolution of human cultures and languages.

Lastly, Epicurus considers how we can best understand heavenly phenomena so as to avoid fear and anxiety and be at peace. Things in the sky are not managed by beings that enjoy perfect bliss. Rather, as with all things, they occur in some natural way. Our happiness depends on the study and understanding of natural phenomena. We must realize that our investigations may only lead to a variety of possible explanations. We should be content with these and not demand single explanations.

Epicurus concludes by urging Herodotus to keep his summary of the nature of things in mind.

THE LETTER TO PYTHOCLES

AFTER GREETING PYTHOCLES, Epicurus happily agrees to satisfy his request for an epitome on things that happen in the sky.

Before getting to these celestial phenomena, Epicurus reminds Pythocles that the whole point of seeking knowledge of anything is to obtain "tranquility of mind and resolute conviction and confidence." He suggests that some things admit one explanation, whereas others, such as things in the sky, allow for multiple explanations. Sometimes we can interpret phenomena by means of our own experiences. Regardless, it is important to keep to the facts alone.

Epicurus first explores the development of the many worlds from the infinite. A world (cosmos) is "a circumscribed portion of the sky" that "contains stars, an earth, and all other visible things." There are an infinite number of worlds that have many different shapes. Worlds develop from prior "seeds."

He goes on to offer various explanations for those things in the sky having to do with the sun, the moon, and other stars—the relative size of the sun and other stars; their rising and setting; why the sun and moon follow particular paths; the waxing and waning of the moon, how it shines, and why a face appears in the moon; eclipses of the sun and moon; and why days and nights vary in length. He later discusses comets ("stars with long hair"), and why some stars appear to move, while others appear to remain still or fall.

Otherwise, he explores how different earthly, atmospheric, and weather phenomena occur—including clouds, rain, thunder, lightning, whirlwinds, earthquakes, winds, hail, snow, dew, frost, ice, rainbows, and lunar halos. He denies that animals foretell weather.

In going through these things, Epicurus' point is two-fold. One, there are many possible explanations for all these phenomena. Two, one should not resort to mythological or any other non-observational accounts in order to explain them. It is important to always keep the ultimate goal of study in mind while making any investigation—the goal of genuine tranquility of mind, of living undisturbed by various feelings, thoughts, and judgments.

THE LETTER TO MENOECEUS

AFTER GREETING MENOECEUS, Epicurus suggests that everyone should study philosophy in order to be happy. One should practice living well by keeping a few key truths in mind and making choices in keeping with these.

The first truth is that the gods are blessed and indestructible and nothing to the contrary. The second is that death means nothing to human beings since death is the loss of all sensation. "When we exist, death is not present, and when death is present, we do not exist." The wise man does not pine for immortality; rather, he seeks merely to enjoy life. And yet—the third truth—we should not seek to satisfy every desire since only the satisfaction of some desires (natural and necessary versus groundless desires) is necessary for happiness. The goal is bodily health and mental tranquility. Therefore, we seek freedom from pain and fear. For this reason, Epicurus discusses the fourth truth of pleasure and pain. Not every pleasure is chosen and not every pain is rejected. Rather, pleasure is only required "when we feel pain due to the absence of pleasure."

The best life is the self-sufficient, simple life centered on natural and necessary desires and trouble-free pleasures. Practical wisdom aids one in living this life, counseling one to live according to the virtues. The wise man freely chooses and practices happiness. In conclusion, Epicurus advises Menoeceus to practice "these matters and related precepts" alone and with others.

GLOSSARY

OF ENGLISH WORDS & GREEK EQUIVALENTS

*that appear in Epicurus' letters and sayings,
and Diogenes Laertius' account of Epicurus*

Accident: *sumbebēkos* (συμβεβηκός) from *sumbainō* (συμβαίνω).*

Advantage, benefit: *sumpheron* (συμφέρον).

Agreement, convention, compact: *sunthēkē* (συνθήκη).

Analogy; correspondence; proportion: *analogia* (ἀναλογία).

Anger, wrath; natural impulse: *orgē* (ὀργή).

Anxiety, worry: *phrontis* (φροντίς).

Apparition: *phantasma* (φάντασμα).

Appetite, desire: *orexis* (ὄρεξις).

Assumption: *hupolēpsis* (ὑπόληψις).

Atom; uncut; uncuttable, indivisible: *atomos* (ἄτομος).

Avoidance, flight, escape: *phugē* (φυγή).

Barley cake: *maza* (μᾶζα).

Benefit, utility, profit, advantage: *ōpheleia* (ὠφέλεια).

Bliss, happiness: *makariotēs* (μακαριότης).

Blessed, happy: *makarios* (μακάριος).

Body; any material substance: *sōma* (σῶμα).

Calming (of the mind): *galēnismos* (γαληνισμός). Spend life calmly: *engalēnizō* (ἐγγαληνίζω).

Chance, luck, fortune: *tychē* or *tuchē* (τύχη).

Choice; a taking for oneself: *hairesis* (αἵρεσις).

Clear, distinct; visible; manifest: *enargēs* (ἐναργής). Clearly perceived phenomenon: *enargēma* (ἐνάργημα). Clear and distinct perception; clear evidence: *enargeia* (ἐνάργεια).

Composite, combination: *sunkrisis* (σύγκρισις).

Confidence, assurance; trust, faith: *pistis* (πίστις).

Confirmation, corroboration: *epimarturēsis* (ἐπιμαρτύρησις).

Contempt, disdain: *kataphronēsis* (καταφρόνησις).

Cosmos, world, universe: *kosmos* (κόσμος).

Courage; manliness, manhood, manly spirit: *andreia* (ἀνδρεία).

Criterion, standard; a means for judging, testing, or trying: *kritērion* (κριτήριον); the plural is *kritēria* (κριτήρια).

Death: *thanatos* (θάνατος).

Desire, yearning, longing: *epithumia* (ἐπιθυμία).

Disturbance, annoyance, distress: *ochlēsis* (ὄχλησις).

Earthquake; shaking: *seismos* (σεισμός).

Easy to get: *euporistos* (εὐπόριστος). Hard to get: *dusporistos* (δυσπόριστος).

Envy, ill-will, jealousy: *phthonos* (φθόνος).

Excellence, virtue, goodness: *aretē* (ἀρετή).

Fact(s), phenomena: *phainomena* (φαινόμενα).

False: *pseudēs* (ψευδής).

Falsehood, untruth, lie: *pseudos* (ψεῦδος).

Fault, failure; sin: *hamartēma* (ἁμάρτημα).

Fear, terror: *phobos* (φόβος).

Feeling; anything that befalls one; what one has suffered, one's experience; of the soul, a passion, emotion; any passive state, a condition: *pathos* (πάθος).

Flesh: *sarx* (σάρξ).

Form, shape: *morphē* (μορφή).

Free, without a master: *adespotos* (ἀδέσποτος). Master: *despotēs* (δεσπότης).

Freedom from pain: *aponia* (ἀπονία).

Friend; dear one: *philos* (φίλος).

Garden (as in Epicurus' garden): *kēpos* (κῆπος).

Goal (of life), end; purpose: *telos* (τέλος).

God, a god: *theos* (θεός). **Gods**: *theoi* (θεοί).

Good cheer, merriment: *euphrosunē* (εὐφροσύνη).

Gratitude, thankfulness: *charis* (χάρις). Gratitude: *eucharistia* (εὐχαριστία).

Groundless: *kenos* (κενός).

Happiness: *eudaimonia* (εὐδαιμονία). Happy: *eudaimōn* (εὐδαίμων).

Harm: *blabē* (βλάβη).

Hate, hatred: *misos* (μῖσος).

Heat (in relation to what the soul resembles): *thermos* (θερμός).

Health, soundness: *hygieia* or *hugieia* (ὑγίεια).

Human organism; an assemblage of atoms: *athroisma* (ἄθροισμα).

Incorporeal: *asōmatos* (ἀσώματος).

Image: *eidōlon* (εἴδωλον).

Immortality: *athanasia* (ἀθανασία).

Impression; the print or impress of a seal: *tupos* (τύπος).

Indestructible: *aphthartos* (ἄφθαρτος). Destroy, ruin: *phtheirō* (φθείρω).

Indifferent, neither good nor bad: *adiaphoros* (ἀδιάφορος).

Infinite, unbounded, unlimited: *apeiros* (ἄπειρος).

Innate, inborn, natural: *sumphutos* (σύμφυτος).

Joy, delight: *chara* (χαρά).

Justice, righteousness: *dikaiosunē* (δικαιοσύνη). **Just**: *dikaios* (δίκαιος). Justly: *dikaiōs* (δικαίως).

Established, static; pertaining to a state or condition (related to pleasure): *katastēmatikos* (καταστηματικός). See static.

Kinetic, motion, movement (related to pleasure): *kinēsis* (κίνησις). Related to *kineō* (κινέω): to set or to be put in motion.

Limit, boundary: *peras* (πέρας).

Living being, animal: *zōon* (ζῷον).

Live well: to live (*zaō*) (ζάω) well or beautifully (*kalōs*) (καλῶς), the adverbial form of beautiful, good, fine, noble: *kalos* (καλός).

Love; desire: *erōs* (ἔρως).

Mind, thought: *dianoia* (διάνοια).

Measure, rule, standard: *kanōn* (κανών). Also: *horos* (ὅρος).

Motion; state of movement: *kinēsis* (κίνησις).

Myth, story: *mythos* or *muthos* (μῦθος).

Natural: *physikos* or *phusikos* (φυσικός).

Nature: *physis* or *phusis* (φύσις).

Necessary: *anankaios* (ἀναγκαῖος).

Necessity, force, constraint: *anankē* (ἀνάγκη).

Noble, beautiful: *kalos* (καλός). Nobly: *kalōs* (καλῶς).

Notion, thought: *epinoia* (ἐπίνοια). A thought, notion, conception: *ennoia* (ἔννοια).

Opinion, notion, judgment, belief, conjecture; teaching: *doxa* (δόξα).

Pain, suffering; grief: *algēdōn* (ἀλγηδών). Pain (of body or mind): *lupē* (λύπη).

Philosophy: *philosophia* (φιλοσοφία). Philosopher; lover of wisdom: *philosophos* (φιλόσοφος). To do or study philosophy: *philosopheō* (φιλοσοφέω).

Place: *chōra* (χώρα).

Pleasure, delight, enjoyment: *hēdonē* (ἡδονή). Pleasant: *hēdus* (ἡδύς).

Practical wisdom: *phronēsis* (φρόνησις).

Practice, attend to; exercise oneself: *meletaō* (μελετάω).

Preconception; a mental picture or scheme into which experience is fitted; general concept: *prolēpsis* (πρόληψις).

Presentation; appearance: *phantasia* (φαντασία).

Property, attribute: *sumptōma* (σύμπτωμα) from *sumpiptō* (συμπίπτω).*

Quality: *poiotēs* (ποιότης).

Reason: *logos* (λόγος). Without reason, non-rational, irrational: *alogos* (ἄλογος).

Safety, personal safety: *asphaleia* (ἀσφάλεια).

Seed: *sperma* (σπέρμα).

Self-sufficiency, independence: *autarkeia* (αὐτάρκεια).

Sensation, sense perception; the senses: *aisthēsis* (αἴσθησις).

Shape, form, figure: *schēma* (σχῆμα).

Simple, frugal, thrifty; easily paid for: *eutelēs* (εὐτελής). Simple, frugal; inexpensive: *litos* (λιτός).

Size, greatness, magnitude: *megethos* (μέγεθος).

Soul: *psychē* or *psuchē* (ψυχή).

Standing; state of rest: *stasis* (στάσις).

Star: *astēr* (ἀστήρ). **Sun**: *hēlios* (ἥλιος). **Moon**: *selēnē* (σελήνη).

Static, established; at rest; katastematic: *katastēmatikos* (καταστημ-ατικός).

Suspicion, worry, ill-feeling: *hupopsia* (ὑποψία).

Thoughtful, reasoning man: *eulogistos* (εὐλόγιστος).

Time: *chronos* (χρόνος).

Tranquility; calmness: *ataraxia* (ἀταραξία). Not disturbed, without confusion; tranquil; calm: *ataraktos* (ἀτάρακτος). Confusion, trouble, disorder, disturbance, anxiety: *tarachos* (τάραχος) or *tarachē* (ταραχή)—thus, the former negate *tarachos* or *tarachē*.

Truth (opposed to mere appearance); reality: *alētheia* (ἀλήθεια).

True; unconcealed; real: *alēthēs* (ἀληθής).

Unchangeable: *ametablētos* (ἀμετάβλητος).

Unclear, obscure; not evident to sense: *adēlos* (ἄδηλος).

Untroubled, without trouble; unperturbed: *athorubos* (ἀθόρυβος).

Virtue; excellence; goodness: *aretē* (ἀρετή).

Void, empty; groundless: *kenos* (κενός).

Water: *hudōr* (ὕδωρ).

Weather phenomena: **Rain**: *hudōr* (ὕδωρ). **Cloud**: *nephos* (νέφος). **Rainbow**: *iris* (ἶρις). **Thunder**: *brontē* (βροντή). **Lightning**: *astrapē* (ἀστραπή). **Snow**: *chiōn* (χιών). **Ice**: *krustallos* (κρύσταλλος). **Hail**: *chalaza* (χάλαζα). **Frost**: *pachnē* (πάχνη).

Weight: *baros* (βάρος) or *barus* (βαρύς).

Wind (in relation to what the soul resembles): *pneuma* (πνεῦμα).

Wisdom: *sophia* (σοφία). Wise man: *sophos* (σοφός).

Wise: *phronimos* (φρόνιμος). Wisely: *phronimōs* (φρονίμως).

Word, speech, sound: *phthongos* (φθόγγος).

World, cosmos, universe: *kosmos* (κόσμος).

Yearning, longing, fond desire: *pothos* (πόθος).

---

* We at The Classics Cave have followed the recent and consistent scholarship of Lloyd P. Gerson (and sometimes Brad Inwood with others) in giving *sumbebēkos* as "accident" and *sumptōma* as "property."

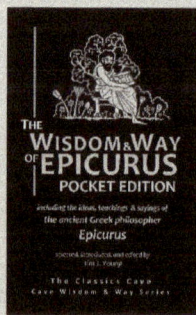

SOURCES & FURTHER READING

This Classics Cave rendition of Epicurus' works and Diogenes Laertius' reflections on Epicurus was made using the critical editions of H. Usener (*Epicurea*, Leipzig, 1887), C. Bailey (*Epicurus*, Oxford, 1926), and that found in R.D. Hicks' translation of Diogenes Laertius (*Diogenes Laertius: Lives of Eminent Philosophers*, Cambridge, 1925), as well as the Greek texts and other immensely helpful tools found online at the Perseus Digital Library (www.perseus.tufts.edu).

Otherwise, The Classics Cave checked its own version against many other translations, new and old, including those of R.D. Hicks (1925), C. Bailey (1926), George K. Strodach (1963), Eugene O'Connor (1993), and Brad Inwood and L.P. Gerson (1994).

Where the translation of the material from or related to Epicurus in the public domain was suitable, The Classics Cave occasionally made use of it with little to no alteration.

OTHER ANCIENT LITERATURE
RELATED TO EPICUREANISM

Lucretius: On the Nature of Things. Translated by W.H.D. Rouse. Cambridge: Harvard University Press, 1924.

FURTHER READING

Copleston, Frederick. *Greece and Rome: From the Pre-Socratics to Plotinus*. Vol. 1 of *A History of Philosophy*. Westminster: Newman Press, 1946.

Dewitt, N.W. *Epicurus and His Philosophy*. Minneapolis: University of Minnesota Press, 1954.

Farrington, Benjamin. *The Faith of Epicurus*. New York: Basic Books, 1967.

Festugiere, Andre-Jean. *Epicurus and His Gods*. Translated by C.W. Chilton. Cambridge: Harvard University Press, 1956.

Frischer, Bernard. *The Sculpted Word: Epicureanism and Philosophical Recruitment in Ancient Greece*. Berkeley: University of California Press, 1982.

Gordon, Dane R. and David B. Suits, eds. *Epicurus: His Continuing Influence and Contemporary Relevance*. Rochester: RIT Cary Graphic Arts Press, 2003.

Gottlieb, Anthony. *The Dream of Reason: A History of Western Philosophy from the Greeks to the Renaissance*. New York: W.W. Norton & Company, 2016.

Grafton, Anthony, Glenn W. Most, and Salvatore Settis, eds. *The Classical Tradition*. Cambridge: The Belknap Press, 2010.

Hadot, Pierre. *What Is Ancient Philosophy?* Translated by Michael Chase. Cambridge: Harvard University Press, 2002.

————. *Philosophy as a Way of Life*. Translated by Michael Chase. Malden: Blackwell Publishing, 1995.

Hibler, Richard. *Happiness through Tranquility: The School of Epicurus*. Lanham: University Press of America, 1984.

Hicks, R.D. *Stoic and Epicurean*. New York: Scribner, 1910.

Kenny, Anthony. *Ancient Philosophy*. Vol. of *A New History of Western Philosophy*. Oxford: Clarendon Press, 2004.

Klein, Daniel. *Travels with Epicurus: A Journey to a Greek Island in Search of a Fulfilled Life*. New York: Penguin Books, 2012.

Long, A.A. *Hellenistic Philosophy: Stoics, Epicureans, Sceptics*. 2nd ed. London: Duckworth, 1986.

Meyer, Susan Sauvé. *Ancient Ethics: A Critical Introduction*. Abingdon: Routledge, 2008.

Rist, J.M. *Epicurus: An Introduction*. Cambridge: Cambridge University Press, 1972.

Taylor, A.E. *Epicurus*. London: Constable & Company, 1911.

Slattery, Luke. *Reclaiming Epicurus: Ancient Wisdom that Could Save the World*. New York: Penguin Books, 2012.

Warren, James, ed. *The Cambridge Companion to Epicureanism*. Cambridge: Cambridge University Press, 2009.

Wilson, Catherine. *Epicureanism: A Very Short Introduction*. Oxford: Oxford University Press, 2015.

Will you help the Cave?

- **Buy** a book. **Join** a club. **Sponsor** the Cave. **Give** a donation.
- **Talk** to friends and family about Cave books and the free online Cave content at the Cave (www.theclassicscave.com).
- Leave a **positive review** online—if possible, **five stars** with a **brief remark** about what you liked. This truly helps!
- **Write us** at contact@theclassicscave.com to let us know how you've benefited from our work. This inspires us to do more!

THE CLASSICS CAVE is a small, shoestring operation, on fire to spread the wisdom and ways of ancient Greek literature. We **rely on you**, the friend of the Cave, to let people know how you liked and benefited from what we're doing. We also **depend on you** to **improve our books**. Did you see something that requires editing? Something we got wrong? Something we need to add? Despite our great effort and care to get everything right, it happens. So please **let us know** by emailing us at contact@theclassicscave.com. Otherwise, **visit** the Cave to benefit from our ever-growing collection of free online content at www.theclassicscave.com. And don't forget to **support our mission** to spread the wisdom and ways of ancient Greek literature by **buying** and **reading** Cave Books, **enjoying** Cave Gear, **joining** The BAGL Club or AAGS, or by **sponsoring** or **giving** to the Cave. **Thanks!**

Read and enjoy more from **Epicurus**!

If you benefited from *The Best of Epicurus*, you may wish to pick up another Cave book related to him and his work. There are a few now available.
Visit the Cave at . . .
www.theclassicscave.com

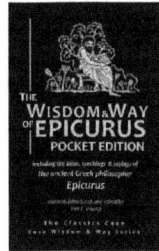

www.theclassicscave.com

Looking for the **best books** ever?

Hunting for **wisdom** and **ways** that
are time-tested and people-approved?

When you read a Cave book, an ancient classic,
you'll have a better idea about where you're
going in life and how to get there.

You'll feel smarter. Be wiser.
And if you practice what you've encountered,
you'll live a better life. Be a little happier.

Enjoy the Cave's **free online content**. Or **choose a book** from one
of **our series**. The Cave Best of Series. The Cave Wisdom & Way Series. The Cave Workbook & Journal Series. And more!
You'll be glad you did!

Pick up a **CAVE** book . . .

from HOMER . . .

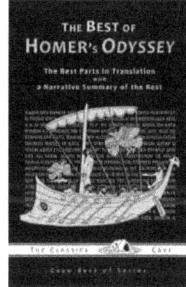

from the CYNICS . . .

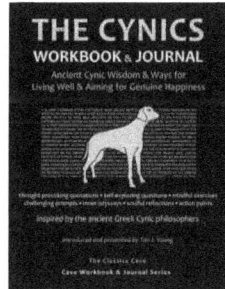

From EPICURUS . . .

www.theclassicscave.com

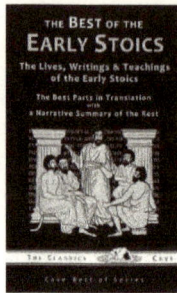

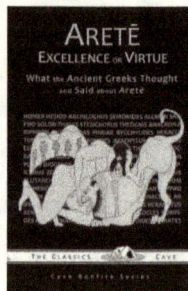